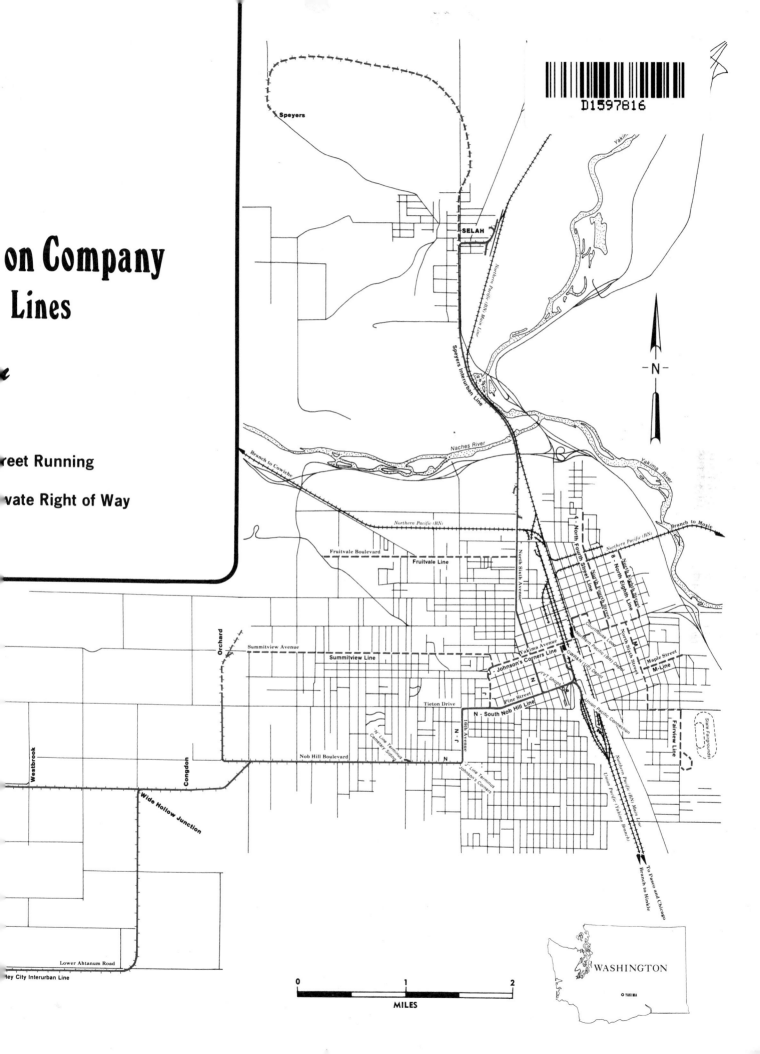

on Company
Lines

reet Running

vate Right of Way

Speyers

SELAH

Northern Pacific (BN) Main Line

Speyers Interurban Line

Branch to Cowiche

Naches River

Yakima River

Branch to Moxie

Northern Pacific (BN)

Fruitvale Boulevard

Fruitvale Line

North Sixth Avenue

North Fourth Avenue

4 - North Fourth Street Line

Northern Pacific (BN)

8 - North Eighth Line

North Sixth Street

Courthouse Loop

Maple Street

Orchard

Summitview Avenue

Summitview Line

OWR&N (UP) Depot

Johnson's Corners Line

Northern Pacific (BN) Depot

Yakima Avenue

Union Pacific Connection

M-Line

Fairview Line

State Fairgrounds

Tieton Drive

Pine Street

YV Shops

Z

N - P

N - South Nob Hill Line

16th Avenue

N

Westbrook

Congdon

Nob Hill Boulevard

N Line Terminus
Cemetery Siding

N Line Terminus
Johnson's Corners

Wide Hollow Junction

Northern Pacific (BN) Main Line

Union Pacific (Yakima Branch)

To Pasco and Chicago
Branch to Hinkle

Lower Ahtanum Road

ley City Interurban Line

N

0   1   2

MILES

WASHINGTON

o YAKIMA

D1597816

GIL REID

APPLE COUNTRY INTERURBAN

...A History of the Yakima Valley Tranportation Company and the Yakima Interurban Trolley Lines

Kenneth G. Johnsen

Golden West Books
· San Marino, California ·

APPLE COUNTRY INTERURBAN

Copyright © 1979 by Kenneth G. Johnsen
All rights reserved
Published by Golden West Books
San Marino, California 91108 U.S.A.
Library of Congress Catalog Card No. 79-15270
I.S.B.N. 0-87095-074-6

Library of Congress Cataloging in Publication Data

Johnsen, Kenneth G.,   1946-
    Apple country interurban.

    Bibliography: p.
    Includes index.
    1. Yakima Valley Transportation Company — History.
    2. Local transit — Washington (State) — Yakima Valley — History.
    3. Yakima, Wash. — History. I. Title.
HE4491.Y35Y3444   385'.5'0979755   79-15270
    ISBN 0-87095-074-6

ACKNOWLEDGMENTS

I have been privileged not only to observe the more recent era of street railway service in Yakima, but also to be a part of the unfolding chain of events that brought about the rebirth of passenger trolley service in Washington's apple country. My heartfelt thanks are extended to Wray Brown on two counts: first, for being *the one* who made a rail enthusiast's crazy dream come true, and second, for opening so many doors beyond which lay what was needed to give this volume substance, illustration, and credibility.

To Robert S. Wilson, who probably knows the YVT railroad to a greater degree than any other person, I am deeply indebted for his encouragement and recollections, and for making available to me his entire photographic collection, as well as the notebooks in which for many years he chronicled the day-by-day history of the YVT.

In the enormous job of reading through all the newspapers contemporary to YVT's early years, I was greatly aided by Bob Lince of Selah, one of the area's foremost historians. He also generously loaned me his photo collection, provided reminiscences of early days, and took me on a tour of YVT's abandoned lines and stations.

My sister-in law, Mrs. Janet Larson, deserves special thanks for the splendid line drawings that accompany the roster. Also thanks go to Gil Reid for the beautiful jacket painting and to Tim Muir for the small sketches. Lawton Gowey was especially helpful in providing me with roster information and early photographs.

It is difficult to adequately express my appreciation for the true friendship, encouragement and help given me by the people of the YVT. These include (alphabetically): Donald (Al) Hammermeister, Bob Jones, Mel Lucas, O. L. (Pat) Potter, Jerry Price, and the late Walt Shoot.

Others who have helped me accumulate information over the years include: Mr. and Mrs. John L. Ainsworth, Miss Judy Ainsworth, Ben Alaimo, Mr. and Mrs. Fred Erickson, L. B. Gibbs, Hilding Larson, and Ms. Nancy Prior of the Washington State Library.

Any story requires a publisher to become a book. I am appreciative of the assistance of Donald Duke, publisher of Golden West Books, for his encouragement and help in acquiring additional photographs and data. He has spent countless hours in layout design to blend the story with illustrations.

For their contributions of photographs or other assistance I am also grateful to: Al Barker, Mr. and Mrs. Paul Class, Harre Demoro, Albert Farrow, Bob Gray, William C. Janssen, Mr. and Mrs. Carl M. Johnsen, Frederick A. Johnsen, Kay Kime of Yakima Federal Savings & Loan, Steve Maguire, George Martin, Mrs. Jo Nashem of the Yakima Valley Museum, John Price, Charles D. Savage, Fred Schneider, Charles Smallwood, Kenneth C. Springirth, Will Whittaker, the staff of the Yakima Public Library, and other fine people of the Yakima valley.

Finally, I would like to acknowledge the inspiration given me in my undergraduate years at the University of Washington by my history professor of several quarters, Dr. Thomas Pressly, who molded my way of thinking about history and showed me the techniques of getting the source of the historical record.

Kenneth G. Johnsen, D.D.S.
Renton, Washington
May 9, 1979

TITLE PAGE ILLUSTRATION

The air is fragrant with the perfume of apple blossoms as Yakima Valley Transportation Company interurban No. 100 stops to pick up city-bound passengers in the rolling orchard country surrounding Yakima. Interurban No. 100 is depicted in its original cream and green livery in this splendid watercolor by Gil Reid.

Golden West Books

P.O. BOX 8136 • SAN MARINO, CALIFORNIA • 91108

4

To Lauri

Arriving passengers on Northern Pacific trains would see this 1910 view of downtown Yakima as their train crossed Yakima Avenue and came to a stop at the depot a half block away. — KENNETH G. JOHNSEN COLLECTION

Foreword

At least two generations of Americans have grown up since the end of the trolley car era. The majority of them have never seen a trolley car, save possibly in a museum. True, a few trolley lines still exist, in some six or seven cities at this writing. In the heyday of the streetcar, however, every self-respecting community boasted at least one such line and more often several.

It must be difficult for present-day Americans to realize how important trolley lines once were. In the earliest years of this century, the automobile was little more than a toy, financially out of reach of most families at a time when 35 cents per hour or less was considered a pretty good wage, and unreliable even for those who could afford one. Moreover, the roads of those years, for the most part rough and unpaved, did little to encourage urban travel in individual vehicles. Most of us depended upon the streetcar and its rural counterpart — the interurban — not only for travel to and from school or work, but for recreational excursions in the evenings and on weekends.

Those days are long gone, and now the trolley car's successor — the bus — carries only a handful of people, except in the largest cities. Until the last two decades, interest in its forerunner was at a low ebb. In the 1960's and 1970's, however, some efforts have been made to preserve remaining specimens of the trolley car in museums, and a number of excellent books about trolleys have been published, some national and international in scope, others describing the specific transport facilities of individual cities or regions. Most of the latter have dealt with major urban centers, such as Chicago, Boston, or Baltimore. The volume you hold in your hands now is of a different order, devoted to the small western town that has been my home for my entire 65-year life span.

Its author, Dr. Johnsen, has developed a close feeling for this community and especially for its local electric railway, in consequence of which he has spent countless hours poring over microfilm reproductions of early-day newspapers and interviewing numerous older residents of Yakima who once worked upon, rode, or observed the cars and tracks of which he writes. His has been a labor of love, and I commend it fully to the reader.

Robert S. Wilson
Yakima, Washington

7

Under the singing overhead trolley wire, electric locomotive No. 298 grinds along West Pine Street as it performs its switching chores. On the right, the old trolley carbarn with a modern day motor coach inside the door. — FRED SCHNEIDER

Table of Contents

Foreword 7

Chapter 1 — False Starts, Financiers, and a 40-Year Franchise 11

Chapter 2 — Now You See It, Now You Don't 15

Chapter 3 — Merry Christmas, Yakima! 17

Chapter 4 — Take Me Out to the Fair 19

Chapter 5 — Winners and Losers 29

Chapter 6 — Interurban Expansion 33

Chapter 7 — Creak Slowly, Old Streetcar 47

Chapter 8 — Interurban Decline 57

Chapter 9 — At Low Ebb 69

Chapter 10 — Streetcar Renaissance 95

Appendix 107

Bibliography 128

Index 129

1

False Starts, Financiers, and a 40-year Franchise

Turn-of-the-century North Yakima (as Yakima, Washington was then known) was a community busting its britches with new growth. In the 15 years since its founding by the Northern Pacific Railway, its population had grown to well over 3,000; it had a telephone system, water works, and power company; it was the official site of the annual Washington State Fair; and, in an 1889 election, it had missed becoming the state's capital by only a narrow margin. Where this burgeoning left off in fact, it continued onward and upward in the minds of numerous leading Yakimans and on the pages of their booster-oriented newspapers. Though its first paved street lay some eight years in the future, Yakima's initial mayor, Edward Whitson, proudly announced in December 1900 that a system of electric street railroads for the Yakima Valley and North Yakima in particular was in the works.

Whitson just happened to own the franchises for the water works and the local power company, and at the dawn of the century such companies thrived on contracts to provide power to budding young street railroads. Although the mayor himself could not put up the capital for the railroad enterprise, certain "Eastern capitalists" would soon start to pour cash into the Valley — and then

stand back as a great system of electric lines took shape.

This reference to Eastern capitalists who, it seemed, could never divulge their identity until some later date, set the tone for future strategy whenever it would be deemed desirable to get people excited about electric railroads: Simply spread rumors that some financiers had visited the Valley and been much taken by its potential, and to a man the populace would shout, "Oh, boy! I want a part of this!" While today's culture would probably consider Whitson's position as mayor, operator of the water and electric utilities, and wheeler and dealer with Eastern investors a conflict of interest at best, turn-of-the-century Yakimans' minds focused on increased growth and the jingle of railroad money in their pockets.

The plutocrats did not materialize that year or next, and Whitson's conception failed to bear fruit. The idea was not dead, however, only hibernating. In 1902 it emerged again in the smoke-filled rooms of the Yakima Commercial Club. The Commercial Club, somewhat analogous to a Chamber of Commerce or modern Visitors and Convention Bureau, was a body of the town's leading businessmen whose primary goal was the promotion of Yakima far and wide. Located in commodious quarters in

11

the Clogg Building on Yakima Avenue, it also served as a social organization within which bigwigs from all of the surrounding valleys could hobnob with each other about politics, farming, horses, etc.

At Whitson's suggestion, the Commercial Club established a "Committee in Charge of the Electric Railroad Project" to advance the plan, survey a route, and — where possible — secure the right-of-way. By July 1902 the committee was reporting good progress, and a line was projected not only to serve Yakima streets, but to run down to Sunnyside in the lower Yakima Valley and up the Ahtanum Valley to the west.

The name proposed for this hoped-for network of electric lines, with estimated trackage of 99 miles, was the Yakima Valley Central Railroad. The anticipated cost of building and equipping it was $700,000 — quite a sizeable amount for a small farm town on the edge of the Washington desert. Where was the money to come from? Oh, that would be raised by public subscription! Assuming Yakima's population had grown to, say, 5,000 by that time, the electric railroad's promoters were expecting every man, woman, and child in the city to subscribe a minimum of $140 each. Therein lay the failure of the 1902 version.

William P. Sawyer, a landowner in the lower Valley, kept the idea afloat, conferring with neighboring farmers and attempting to convince them it would be in their common interest to have an electric line connecting their farms with downtown North Yakima. Sawyer believed that the great quantities of produce emanating from the lower Valley would justify the expense of building such a line, and the year 1905 found him writing enthusiastic letters on the subject to the editor of the *Yakima Herald.*

In 1906 the groundwork for what would eventually become the Yakima Valley Transportation Company was laid. The men behind this push were for the most part the same ones who had been involved earlier, and the impetus was channeled once again through the Commercial Club. As before, financing the project constituted the major hurdle. Since the good people of North Yakima tended to hang on to their purse strings, a little positive emphasis on the inherent wisdom of investing in this venture was going to be necessary to get them to open up. Perhaps some testimonials from well-heeled Eastern financiers would awaken the local citizenry to the great opportunity that was knocking.

Thus local newspapers during 1906 headlined no fewer than six different Eastern capitalists who ostensibly had made the overland trip to Yakima to inspect the Valley and its potential.

Some of these nabobs preferred to remain anonymous, e.g., the gentleman who, according to the *Herald,* was "introduced by prominent financiers of the East, visited the city recently, and is suspected to be connected with the James J. Hill (Northern Pacific Railway) interests." He announced that he "would gladly put up $100,000 bond (at some unspecified future date) to the city council to prove he would build an electric line."

Others did have names, e.g. R. E. Allen "of Spokane and Walla Walla," who investigated the Yakima Valley and "deemed it ready for an electric railroad." And one day, a David E. Gould stepped off the Northern Pacific train in Yakima and let the news leak out that he was on a mission from Boston to get an electric railroad system started in the Yakima Valley. Though insisting he was not at liberty to name his backers, he nevertheless contended that they were all "prominent names in big business, well known to the people of the Yakima Valley," and on May 7, 1906 he applied to the city council for a street railway franchise.

If all this was calculated to awaken North Yakimans to investment opportunity, it also had the effect of arousing them to efforts to finance a line locally rather than allow outside interests to control it. At the time, North Yakima was very much at the mercy of the Northern Pacific Railway, which had built the town and successfully blocked attempts by other railroads to enter it. The townspeople resented this monopoly and looked eagerly to new routes being surveyed by the Milwaukee Road and the North Coast Railway. Yakimans were wary of financiers "suspected of being connected with the James J. Hill interests," and some even put forth new pledges to build the street railroad with local funds.

The franchise D. E. Gould applied for was well thought out and favorable to him and his backers. It included the right to build a street railway on "all streets, avenues, and public places" within the city. Gould would not be required to have more than two miles of railroad in operation by July 1908, some two years distant. Responsibility for grading streets not already graded would lie with the city, not the railroad. As a result, Yakima's city fathers could point to the application with alarm: "Are we going to let outsiders come in and control the affairs of our street railroad the way the Northern Pacific controls our commerce with the rest of the country?" The city council announced it would delay action on Gould's application until it had a local petition it could consider simultaneously.

On or about June 2, 1906 a meeting of interested citizens was called at the Commercial Club,

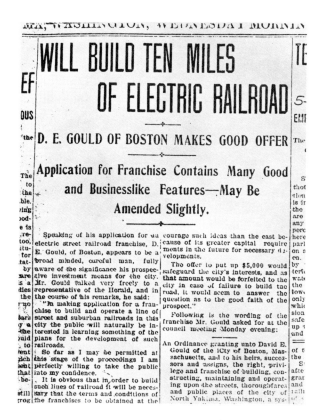

Electric railroad schemes made headlines in Yakima in 1906. Whether it was a local proposal or offers by Eastern financiers, the newspapers buzzed with excitement about street railroads for Yakima. — KENNETH G. JOHNSEN COLLECTION

and a new committee was established to hammer out a franchise proposal. Its five members included W. A. Bell, W. B. Dudley, D. E. Lesh, H. B. Scudder, and I. H. Dills. From the council, these prominent citizens expected — and received — favored status. While the committee's application for a local franchise was in the making, the newspapers — always a helpful tool to those seeking public support or condemnation of enterprises — were rife with rumors and comments about it. The press saw in the proposal "an effort to protect local interests rather than to make money." Keep the base of power in the hands of local residents, and all would be well!

By June 15 the franchise application was almost ready, and another meeting was called at the Commercial Club. Those who attended that summer morning were prominent citizens from Yakima and several of the valleys nearby. The topic for the assemblage: formal organization of the Yakima Inter-Valley Traction Company. This new railway was incorporated by a group of 20 men, and to steer it onto the right track, seven of them — namely, the previously-listed Committee of Five plus A. J. Splawn and Alexander Miller — were to

serve for six months as trustees. In addition to those seven, the group of 20 included P. A. Ditter, W. W. Robertson, James H. Fraser, F. K. Hiscock, M. B. Miles, William P. Sawyer, M. W. Phillips, H. H. Lombard, S. J. Cameron, Miles Cannon, E. J. Jaeger, W. L. Lemon, and Wallace Wiley. Henry B. Scudder was named president of the company and W. A. Bell its manager.

Had a Yakima "Who's Who" in real estate and banking existed in 1906, it undoubtedly would have duplicated the foregoing list. The trustees issued a brief statement to the press to the effect that they did not want the franchise given away to outside interests and hence had formed a local corporation. On June 18, at the regular Monday night meeting of the city council, the Yakima Inter-Valley Traction Company submitted its formal petition for a franchise. The council, obviously pleased, promised early consideration of the matter. It pointed out to the trustees that Selah Street (now North First Avenue) had already been given over in franchise to the Northern Pacific Railway, and also that any franchise given to street railways would prohibit the use of steam power on Yakima streets. Neither condition, however, posed any problem for the petitioners.

With Gould's application in one hand and that of the Yakima Inter-Valley Traction Company in the other, the city council then began a legal study of both. Gould's application was somewhat exacting in its adherence to his own interests, and the council's lawyers suggested a number of amendments that would enhance the city's position. Whether these changes were intended to give Gould a fair chance at the franchise or were prompted by backers of the local scheme as a means of eliminating competition is matter for conjecture. At any rate, Gould did not agree to them, and his application was denied.

After more than three months of study, the council drew up the final version of the franchise it would offer to the Yakima Inter-Valley Traction Company. As might have been expected, it proved more favorable to the city than the Gould proposal and included the following salient features:

The Yakima Inter-Valley Traction Company, "hereinafter called the grantee," could build, operate, and maintain a street railway on all Yakima streets except Naches and Selah.

Franchise would be in effect for 40 years, and grantee must have three miles of railroad in operation by January 1, 1908; seven miles in operation by January 1, 1910; and ten miles in operation by January 1, 1912.

Construction must begin within 90 days of the granting of the franchise.

Grantee must post a $5,000 bond to guarantee its solvency.

Within one year, grantee must file a map with the city clerk showing all streets on which it proposed to operate. Any street not so designated would be "up for grabs" by any other railway.

Height, size, and spacing of poles were prescribed, even though electricity had not been specified as the power source. Any power source other than steam would be permitted.

Streets, whether paved or dirt (at this time Yakima still had no paved roads), were to be maintained flush with the railhead between rails and 18 inches on either side at company expense.

No passing tracks would be permitted on Yakima Avenue, though a double track line would be permitted on any street.

Whenever the city "macadamized" (paved with gravel and oil) a street, grantee would bear the cost of "macadamizing" its portion of the roadway unless the paving was done before the track was laid.

City gave grantee the right to cross any other railway in the city and also reserved the right to allow any other railroad to cross that of the grantee.

City council retained the right to regulate the rates of speed of street railway cars.

Fares were prescribed: Five cents for any adult on a one-way trip within city limits; half-fare for school children going to and from school. (In our age of acceptance of inflation, it seems strange that the company would allow its fares to be exactly spelled out for a 40-year period!)

City officials, policemen, and firemen would be carried free.

After ten years, the city would begin collecting taxes on grantee's equipment.

Headquarters, shops, and offices of the street railway (not surprisingly!) were to remain forever in Yakima.

Passed as an ordinance on Monday, October 1, 1906, the franchise was sent to Mayor Walter J. Reed for signature. Reed vetoed it. His reasons for doing so were not recorded, but a reporter from the *Yakima Republic* assigned to cover council doings wrote that "the mayor was more friendly to the Northern Pacific Railway than to any local combination." Given the immense economic power wielded by the Northern Pacific in comparison to the new and unproven corporation, this contention seems plausible. Two weeks later, however, on October 15, 1906, the council overrode the veto, and the Yakima Inter-Valley Traction Company had its franchise.

2

Now You See It, Now You Don't

Yakima's electric street railroad was born in the heyday of such systems. Similar lines were springing up all over the state and nation. Western Washington already had a number of street railways, and Spokane and Walla Walla in eastern Washington were each in the process of building an electric transportation network. So many electric interurban lines were intimately linked to real estate developments that it was sometimes difficult to know whether a tract had been planned to be near an electric line or an electric line had been built for the purpose of opening up new housing.

Yakima's streetcar promoters never laid claim to any motivation other than providing convenient transit service to city dwellers and connecting the outer areas of the Valley with the inner city. During 1906 and 1907, however, as the electric railroad began to take shape, such names as Scudder, Lesh, and Whitson turned up frequently in advertisements for property "on the route of the new car line." Indeed, why Yakima's entrepreneurs wanted a local traction company they could control is not difficult to surmise.

The railroad offered an issue of $500,000 in common stock for sale in lots of $2,500. The stock was to be subscribed by astute local investors, who would then pay off their portions in assessments collected by the company at various intervals. Yakima Inter-Valley Traction Company reports glowed with enthusiasm as shares were spoken for. By December 1906 about $107,500 had already been subscribed, and prospects "were greater at this time than the manipulators of the scheme anticipated." The company now had 41 stockholders, with "others clamoring . . . for a share." The first assessment, in the amount of three percent, was collected on December 8.

Those clamoring for a share apparently began to lose interest, though, for as 1907 dawned sales of stock declined. William P. Sawyer, ever one of the enterprise's most ardent backers, traveled to the surrounding towns to try to entice regional businessmen to invest, but only a trickle of subscriptions continued to come in. Not one trustee or stockholder in the Yakima Inter-Valley Traction Company had previously been involved in this type of venture. They now began to realize that in their inexperience they had set up an unviable entity. Their lawyers pointed out that until its stock was fully subscribed, the company could not obtain loans.

With well over $300,000 to be collected, prospects for becoming a paid-up undertaking appeared dim. This was the period in time when the greatest amount of capital was needed to finance right-of-way, track materials, and equipment; yet the company could not even legally float a loan, let alone live off its assessments. The board of directors voted to reduce the capital stock to $250,000 in hopes this amount could be fully subscribed — a decision that could not be implemented, because to reduce the amount of a capital stock issue was illegal.

Next the idea of organizing a new, but otherwise identical, company with $250,000 in capital stock — to which the franchise and assets could be turned over — was put forth. The new company, upon full subscription, could make loans in the form of bonds and thus pay its way. The lawyers pointed out, however, that bonds could be issued for no more than double the amount of capital stock. Such a company would therefore not possess adequate borrowing power.

The public, meanwhile, was beginning to wonder about Yakima's street railway. Six months had elapsed since the granting of the franchise, and there was still no sign of construction. Rumors that the company was in the process of selling out to the ubiquitous Eastern capitalists began to circulate. President Scudder issued a number of public statements intended to quell them. "Streetcars would be running by Fair time," he promised. "Construction is about to begin." Routes were outlined, and plans to run the track around the soldiers' monument on Yakima Avenue were publicized in detail. "Rails have been ordered from the East." "Construction is expected to begin shortly." "We are in earnest about building this electric railroad." Still, no visible evidence appeared.

To confound matters further, another issue was taking shape that tended to undermine Scudder and the street railway. Promoters of Yakima's first street paving project, Yakima Avenue, were demanding action. For years, merchants along the Avenue had decried the lack of street sophistication, and they wanted to wait no longer for the muddy thoroughfare to be transformed into a beautifully clean paved street. If the railway were built before the street was paved, the railroad — under the terms of its franchise — would have to pay for the paving of its right-of-way. On the other hand, if the street were paved before the railway was constructed, the city would have to assume all costs of the paving job.

Yakima's mayor and city council, reacting to pressure from Yakima Avenue businessmen, criticized Scudder for foot dragging, insisted that construction could easily begin at once, and implied that Yakima Inter-Valley Traction was simply waiting until the street had been paved, so as to avoid remitting its portion of the cost. To be fair to Scudder, this was not the primary reason for the delay. Lack of money was. The necessary capital simply was not there. The president himself and most of the men involved with the company were so completely unversed in such matters that they were having to learn a number of crucial lessons the hard way. It began to appear that the only solution was to start all over.

On Wednesday morning, June 26, 1907, Scudder called a meeting of trustees in his office. Together they devised a plan labeled acceptable by company lawyers. A new railroad, the Yakima Valley Transportation Company, would be organized with capital stock of $500,000. The existing company would trade all of its physical assets, right-of-way, and franchise for $250,000 of the new company's stock. The stockholders of the Yakima Inter-Valley Traction Company would transfer all of their shares of stock in that company to the Yakima Valley Transportation Company, to be managed by a trustee. In this way they would not be getting something for nothing by retaining stock interest in both companies. The remaining capital stock, it was figured, would be sold by public subscription. The reasoning was that $250,000 would be easier to fully subscribe than $500,000, yet in the end the company would in effect have $500,000 paid-up stock on which to take out loans. To say the least, a pretty clever maneuver!

A. J. (Jack) Splawn was elected president of the newly-formed company, replacing H. B. Scudder. The latter departed the street railway project somewhat under fire and, consequently, feeling bitter about the whole program. Besides President Splawn the Yakima Valley Transportation Company board of trustees included J. O. Cull; Dr. C. G. Fletcher; Alexander Miller; J. H. Rose; W. P. Sawyer; and George S. Rankin, the new general manager. Its first official meeting was held on the evening of July 2, 1907 at the Trust Company Bank's offices. There President Splawn vowed to push the rapid completion of the car line even if to do so might mean bringing in outside capital. He declared he would not serve as president unless all trustees concurred with him in that regard. Unanimously they agreed that they did, and the meeting took on an air of determination and rather jubilant dedication to the new enterprise. The trustees drank a toast, and the history of the Yakima Valley Transportation Company began.

3

Merry Christmas, Yakima!

Completion in mid-August 1907 of the official transfer of Yakima Inter-Valley Traction Company stock certificates and franchise to the Yakima Valley Transportation Company paved the way for construction of the electric railway to begin at last. General Manager Rankin journeyed to Seattle and Tacoma in search of available materials. Eastern suppliers had been extremely slow to ship rails and other equipment, and the January 1, 1908 deadline for three miles of operating railroad was too close for comfort. While Rankin was on the coast, President Splawn was dickering with the city council. Controversy centered again on the paving of Yakima Avenue. Splawn announced that girder rails (with a U-channel for wheel flanges) for use in paved streets had been ordered, but would not arrive in Yakima in time to meet the January 1 deadline. He asked that paving of the Avenue be delayed until the following year, knowing full well that the council wanted the job done at once.

Sensing that this might be an attempt by Yakima Valley Transportation to get out of paying for its share of the paving project, the council said, in effect, "Nothing doing! You lay whatever kind of rails you've got and then replace them with the girder rails when they get here." Splawn

countered that he could not spare rails for such a purpose, and suggested that the city either leave an unpaved strip down the middle of Yakima Avenue or else grant him an extension of the franchise's time limit, sure that the council would be willing to do neither. The result was a verbal stalemate.

In the meantime, Rankin had found some secondhand car and powerhouse equipment on the coast which could serve temporarily until the already-ordered new equipment arrived. From Seattle he secured a dynamo to convert alternating current to direct current to energize the overhead wire. From the Tacoma Railway & Power Company he obtained options to lease two out-of-service single-truck streetcars which had recently been replaced by larger cars.

On September 9, 1907, ground-breaking ceremonies were held at the W. H. Redmon place, to the west of town. About 35 people comprised the construction force that now began building the Yakima Valley Transportation Company railroad. As the deadline for completion of the first three miles of track drew closer, the size of the work force increased. By the beginning of November there were 65 men at work on the track and overhead, and by mid-December almost 100 were on the job. Since the paving of Yakima Avenue remained a stumbling block, the first three miles of line ran from a point on the Avenue just west of the Northern Pacific track (about Second Avenue) out to 12th Avenue, then south to Division Avenue (now Tieton), west to Miles Avenue (now 16th), south to Johnson's Corners, and then west to a terminus on what is now Nob Hill Boulevard. Newspapers reacted with enthusiasm as the line actually became a reality. Daily reports of construction progress aroused excitement, as well as relief. Yakima was really going to get a streetcar system after all!

Rankin had requested that the two Tacoma streetcars be loaded on flatcars and shipped to Yakima during the first week of December. The cars bore Tacoma Nos. 18 and 36 and retained those designations throughout their Yakima Valley Transportation service. Delivered about December 8, they were quickly unloaded and placed on Yakima Valley Transportation tracks. The diminutive single-truck cars must have looked tiny to Yakimans, because the railway promptly went to great lengths to explain that they were only temporary cars, that bigger and better new ones were on order and would soon arrive from the East. (Actually the equipment on order was approximately the same size.)

By December 21, just ten days short of the deadline, finishing touches were being applied to the first three miles of track and overhead wire. No sidings or passing tracks had yet been installed, and only a rudimentary primary line of track was now declared operable. Sunday, December 22 saw the first — though unofficial — movement of an electric streetcar in Yakima. Once short running tests of both cars had been made to determine the system's operational worthiness, everything was ready. Public runs were to begin at 2:00 P.M. on Christmas Day, following an "inaugural special" trip on Christmas Eve.

Local papers hailed Yakima Valley Transportation's Christmas gift to Yakima, and Splawn and the company's trustees became the heroes of the hour. In the early afternoon of December 24 some 35 excited people crowded into the former's office at First and B Streets. Invited guests for the first official run included the company directors, the members of the city council, and the former directors of the Yakima Inter-Valley Traction Company, as well as several newspapermen. The atmosphere was one of gala celebration as President Splawn briefed the gathering on the road's accomplishments to date. He then proudly led the group on a walking tour of Yakima Valley Transportation's physical plant, which at that time included one small dynamo and a single repair pit,

The first streetcar to turn a wheel on the YVT was Tacoma Railway & Power No. 18. This car and No. 36 were employed for about ten months. — LAWTON GOWEY COLLECTION

both without roof or walls to house them! Indeed, the streetcars themselves were forced to endure outdoor storage initially. The mud at that point on Yakima Avenue was deep enough to cause most of the trolley officials to wear high boots.

The proud citizens touring the facility recognized only accomplishment as they gazed at the machinery and pit. Visions of a big-city public transportation system must have danced through their heads while Splawn spoke on in eloquent terms of the coming grandeur of the Yakima Valley Transportation Company. The guests then climbed aboard Car No. 18. Once they had seated themselves, Splawn took the controls and the trolley trundled off to the cheers of a multitude of bystanders. The newspaper reporters reached hyperbole. The line was "as smooth as glass," wrote one. People all down the line "cheered and threw their hats into the air" as the trolley rolled by.

Three miles and 14 minutes later, at the Wide Hollow end of the track, all passengers "alighted and walked some distance to gain a better view of the proposed extension of the line" to the west. The president of the railroad had thoughtfully brought along a box of Havana cigars, and now passed them out to all the celebrants. After more glowing speeches, and some patting of backs, the inaugural party reboarded the official car and rode back to the beginning of the line, thrilled at what had finally come to pass. For their part, the reporters rushed back to their typewriters and began to bang out stories for the following day's editions. Predictably, the first run received full-width front-page headlines. The Yakima Valley Transportation Company railroad was now ready for business.

18

4

Take Me Out to the Fair

The regular fare on the new Yakima streetcar was five cents, but passengers could purchase six tickets for 25 cents or 25 tickets for one dollar. On opening day, December 25, 1907, the Yakima Valley Transportation Company collected 1,320 fares. The single car in operation completed a round trip every 40 minutes, and most trips were jammed far beyond normal capacity. Until a passing track was built, however, only one car at a time could function. Weekend runs were especially crowded, with proud townspeople, large families, dainty elderly ladies, and an assortment of gawkers all out for a grand ride. The popularity of the new attraction and public eagerness to ride the trolleys remained at high pitch until well into the new year of 1908.

Patronage was off to a good start, but stock subscriptions continued to lag. Once again it was time to dust off a few Eastern financiers and parade them around town to show the citizenry that moneyed people were interested in Yakima's transit system. Thus there appeared once more in the papers a series of individuals spreading the message: "Wait 'til word of Yakima's electric railroad hits the East Coast! Why, investors will snap up this stock in no time!" The push for stock subscriptions now assumed greater proportions

than in 1906. Yakima Valley Transportation placed large ads in the regional papers offering a "conservative investment with small capital . . . call on President Splawn or Secretary Miles in their offices and talk it over." Purchasing had been facilitated. No longer did stock have to be bought in lumps of $2,500. A mere $50 could make its astute investor a shareholder in the Yakima Valley Transportation Company.

William Sawyer was eternally optimistic about the possibility of raising the needed finances at home. Jack Splawn and General Manager George Rankin, however, were perhaps more closely attuned to the practical limits of North Yakima's investing capabilities. While the stock purchase campaign was being fervently waged at the local level Splawn sent Rankin and company attorney J. O. Cull to the East Coast to hunt for financial backing. They returned home the first week of July and reported on a promising top secret deal with a syndicate. Apparently this "deal" fell through, for within a few months Yakima Valley Transportation was looking elsewhere for expansion capital.

Throughout 1908 work on track extensions continued. The crossing frogs needed on Yakima Avenue — for crossing the Northern Pacific's

main line — arrived, and an agreement for their installation was worked out with the steam railroad. At this time the Northern Pacific had eight tracks across Yakima Avenue, no two pair of which were at the same level. It agreed to regrade all of them and to install the trolley crossing at its own convenience and bill Yakima Valley Transportation for the job.

By late March the girder rails were still undelivered and Yakima Avenue was still unpaved. Nevertheless, the city fathers now saw fit to enact Yakima's first speed limits. Vehicles on Yakima Avenue and two blocks to either side were restricted to six miles per hour, and those on country roads to a breakneck 24 miles per hour. These limits applied not only to Yakima's fledgling trolleys, but to "horses, automobiles, motorcycles, and flying machines." Not long after the passage of this far-sighted legislation, toward the end of April, the girder rails were delivered. Suddenly Yakima merchants found themselves watching the steady advance of streetcar tracks down the east end of Yakima Avenue in front of their establishments. While the Avenue would eventually be double-tracked, only the northernmost of the two tracks was laid at this time. During the summer the Northern Pacific completed its installation of the crossing frogs, thus connecting the eastern Yakima Avenue rails with the western end of the line. September 7, 1908 marked the first crossing of the Northern Pacific tracks and the opening up of Yakima's east side to trolley service.

A Yakima Valley Transportation Co. construction train on Yakima Avenue during the summer of 1908 and prior to the stringing up of overhead wires. This 0-4-0 steam locomotive was purchased secondhand, and went on to help in the construction of the North Coast Railway when it entered Yakima a few years later. — GEORGE M. MARTIN COLLECTION

The postcard view on the left is the earliest known photograph of a streetcar in Yakima. It looks east on Yakima Avenue from Front Street. Note that Tacoma Railway & Power No. 18 has a tower mounted on the roof which was used for work on the overhead wire. — YAKIMA VALLEY MUSEUM COLLECTION (BELOW) By the summer of 1908, the YVT rails finally crossed the Northern Pacific main line tracks at the depot on Yakima Avenue. — GEORGE M. MARTIN COLLECTION

Yakima Avenue in the halcyon days of street railway service when the single-truck YVT trolleys were the last word in modern transit. This view is looking east, and many of these buildings still stand today. — YAKIMA FEDERAL SAVINGS & LOAN COLLECTION

Improvements in Yakima Valley Transportation's physical plant also took place that year. The arrival of its new powerhouse dynamo caused an exuberant but somewhat uninformed *Republic* reporter to tell his readers that "the company's own motor, of 200 horsepower, is now here and will be at once harnessed to the current, or have the current harnessed to it, or whatever it is that happens." The three new built-for-Yakima trolleys arrived on September 16 from the Danville Car Company of Danville, Illinois aboard Northern Pacific flatcars. They were slightly more modern and certainly shinier than the ex-Tacoma cars. The sides of these cars, Nos. 1, 2, and 3, were handsomely lettered "Yakima Valley Transportation Company." General Manager Rankin fairly beamed as he showed off his new beauties.

Yakima Valley Transportation Company's first time table was published in the local newspaper for every one to see. — KENNETH G. JOHNSEN COLLECTION (BE-LOW) Looking down Yakima Avenue in 1909, a street completely void of automobiles. At the time it was the only paved road in town. In the distance another YVT car can be seen approaching. It will turn onto the North Fourth Street Line before it reaches the trolley in the foreground. — LAWTON GOWEY COLLECTION

Motorman and conductor aboard one of the original Danville cars pose before departing for Maple Street. Little wooden shelters, such as the one seen at the left, kept winter's snow off waiting passengers. — KENNETH G. JOHNSEN COLLECTION (LEFT) Scene along the North Fourth Street Line in the snow. The YVT did not have a snow sweeper and its trolleys had to make their way as best they could. — YAKIMA SAVINGS & LOAN COLLECTION

The men who built the Yakima Valley Transportation Company pose for this official portrait in 1913. They are, standing left to right: Howard C. Lucas, A.E. Larson, William P. Sawyer, and William Bell. Seated, left to right: A. J. "Jack" Splawn, Alexander Miller, and George Rankin. — FRED ERICKSON COLLECTION

"They are the latest and best cars of their size made anywhere," he boasted, "and the company officers are taking a great deal of pride in exhibiting them. They cost about $10,000." Two of the trolleys were put into service immediately. The third had suffered fire damage in one of its vestibules, owing to an errant cinder from one of the steam locomotives bringing it to Yakima. After undergoing minor repairs it was put to work the following week.

Buffalo Bill Cody's Wild West Show happened to be playing Yakima at this time, and the new

End of the line and turn around point of the North Fourth Street Line. Here the motorman alighted and pulled the trolley pole around to the other end of the car. Highwaymen often took advantage of this situation at night and robbed the motorman and hapless passengers aboard the streetcar. — LAWTON GOWEY COLLECTION

Yakima Avenue was the only YVT line that was double-tracked. The North Fourth Street Line veers off to the right in this view. The trolley in the distance is about to cross the Northern Pacific tracks near Front Street. Here the double track became single while crossing the NP line. — YAKIMA FEDERAL SAVINGS & LOAN COLLECTION

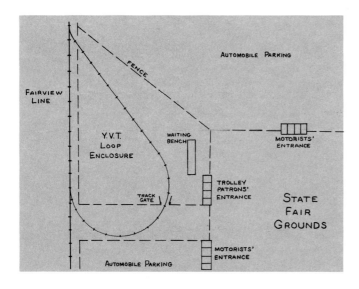

A loop was installed at the State Fair Grounds to assist in crowd control. The notice at the right was published in the newspaper in 1910. - KENNETH G. JOHNSEN

The Washington State Fair never failed to produce a big surge in patronage. A special loading-unloading loop was constructed with special gates to let people into the fairgrounds directly from the trolleys. In this view, three single-truck cars approach the grounds as express motor No. 300 pulls away with a string of four bench-equipped flatcars, headed back to town for more fairgoers. — BOB LINCE COLLECTION

streetcars put in their first revenue miles hauling spectators across town to the eastern end of track, from where it was a short walk to the circus grounds (now a junior high school site) encampment of the famous cowboy's troupe. Whereas Buffalo Bill's show merely brought in a little extra in fares to the new traction company, the Washington State Fair which opened on September 28, 1908 placed a real strain on the system. All five cars (Nos. 1, 2, 3, 18, and 36) were pressed into service for its duration.

Special trains brought in fairgoers from far and wide to the Northern Pacific depot near Yakima Avenue. There they boarded Yakima Valley Transportation Company trolleys for the ride out to the fairgrounds. Washingtonians from all over the state flocked to this annual event, and Yakimans were proud to have their traction system in operation for the visitors. Taking one of the new streetcars to the fair was an activity in no way to be missed. It lent an additional fillip to the gaiety of "fair time," the gala phenomenon that marked the end of summer's harvest in so many American locales well on into the 20th century.

The 1908 edition of the Washington State Fair included, in addition to the regular exhibits, races, and stock shows, a pickled 100-ton whale and an uncommonly large display of new-fangled gasoline-powered engines. About the only attraction that drew larger crowds than the gasoline engines was bristly old Ezra Meeker, the early-day pioneer from Puyallup, who had driven his team of oxen over the mountains to Yakima just for the occasion. Pickpockets had a field day, not only at the fairgrounds but working the crowded trolleys. Their ploy was to start a commotion in one end of a car, and while the riders' attentions were thus diverted make a fast touch. Literally hundreds of dollars in cash and jewels were lost in this fashion.

Riders were admonished not to get on or off a streetcar while it was in motion, and not to ride in the vestibule section, on the fender, or on the roof! When it was all over, the five Yakima Valley Transportation Company streetcars had carried 35,000 fairgoers without a single accident and only one mishap. On September 29 an electrical problem had fouled the dynamo, causing all trolley service to be shut down for the day. With that many riders safely transported, the management gave a justified sigh of relief.

This postcard view taken during the late 1910's shows a newcomer to Yakima Avenue — the gasoline-powered automobile. Dramatic changes were soon to be wrought by this newcomer, and the YVT would feel its effects faster than anyone expected. — LAWTON GOWEY COLLECTION

5

Winners and Losers

George Donald and Robert Strahorn were railroad builders. In the early 1900's their names were probably closer to the front of most Yakimans' minds than even that of President Teddy Roosevelt, for these two entrepreneurs were assiduously buying up rights-of-way in the Yakima Valley. Donald was building the North Yakima & Valley Railroad up the Naches and other valleys. That he was a puppet of the Northern Pacific Railway was a common assumption, although no one could point to any specific evidence to prove it. He had been one of the builders of the Northern Pacific when it passed through the Yakima Valley en route to Tacoma and had subsequently settled in North Yakima. Strahorn was constructing — or rather claimed he soon would construct — the North Coast Railway on a route from the Columbia River via the lower Yakima Valley to Yakima. Many hoped this railroad would eventually cross the snowy Cascade Mountains to Seattle and other Puget Sound cities, thereby becoming a direct competitor of the Northern Pacific. Strahorn had been a somewhat familiar figure around Yakima since 1903, when he arrived from Spokane and bought out Edward Whitson's power and water franchises. Just who was backing his North Coast Railway venture was a matter of consider-

able local speculation.

Donald's North Yakima & Valley Railroad was planned as a network of feeder lines from outlying districts to the hub of North Yakima. Strahorn's line represented a direct link between the Columbia River (and, incidentally, the Union Pacific's Oregon Railway & Navigation Company) and Yakima (and possibly points beyond). At Union Gap, which separates the lower Yakima Valley from its upper regions, these two projects clashed head-on. Each builder desired to keep the other out of the gap, and for a time both were working feverishly to secure a right-of-way and survey a route through it.

Opposing survey crews functioned within sight of each other, literally running from location to location, and in their efforts to purchase the required right-of-way Donald and Strahorn were operating only a few steps ahead of them. This horse race competition continued right up to the gap itself. Here George Donald managed to buy a key piece of land, control of which would be absolutely essential to the railroad line that passed through the gap. His purchase would seem to have ended the battle, but it did not. Strahorn, undaunted, lit a fire under his survey team and got it to the crucial acreage ahead of Donald's. By law

Electric locomotive No. 299 was Superintendent Walter Howard's answer to YVT's growing freight business. This engine was purchased from a Union Pacific subsidiary line in Oregon. Unfortunately, the engine had a tendency to slip when coupled to a heavy load. To remedy this, hunks of scrap iron were placed on the pilot beams on each end of the body. The engine is shown here on Pine Street in 1921. — ROBERT S. WILSON

the surveyor of a route was allowed to sue in court for condemnation of the land for right-of-way purposes. Strahorn proceeded to do so successfully, thus snatching victory from defeat.

Although actual construction of the North Coast Railway was still a couple of years ahead, Strahorn had now entered North Yakima, to the chagrin of the Northern Pacific. His accomplishment was cheered by monopoly-weary Yakimans; but their jubilation was tempered by a growing curiosity and skepticism as to who was behind Mr. Strahorn. Theories were advanced in the local press, as well as on the streets of Yakima. Many suspected that Harriman of the Union Pacific was the moving hand. Some suggested the Milwaukee Road or the Great Northern. Still others believed the Northern Pacific itself was financing Strahorn. The list of possibilities continued to grow until it included the Chicago & North Western, the Canadian Pacific, and the Soo Line. Even Standard Oil was a suspect! As it turned out, Strahorn was an agent of the Oregon Railway & Navigation Company (a Union Pacific subsidiary). That is getting ahead of the story, however.

After the 1908 State Fair service on the Yakima Valley Transportation Company railroad was cut back to two cars, with three cars operating during the rush hours. In October the two rented streetcars were loaded aboard flatcars and returned to Tacoma. A temporary wooden carbarn was erected at Sixth and Maple Streets, but beyond that Yakima Valley Transportation construction and expansion stabilized. The spring of 1909 found rudimentary beginnings of construction on the North 4th Street line, but little if any indication that the company would have a total of seven miles of track operable by January 1, 1910. The Yakima Valley Transportation Company, therefore, was in danger of having to forfeit its franchise.

One final desperate push for stock subscriptions was undertaken. The *Yakima Herald* jumped into the ring with a number of editorial appeals for someone to come forth "and save the day" by raising the needed capital locally, and a few more Eastern capitalists of course gave the effort their hearty endorsements. A number of additional stock subscriptions did come in, but not enough to change the picture. The handwriting had been on the wall all along. Splawn knew that and Rankin was soon to realize it. Outside financing represented their only hope. The pair turned to Strahorn and his still-secret backer, the Oregon Railway & Navigation Company.

Early in 1909 Oregon Railway & Navigation sent a shrewd young lawyer from Baker, Oregon to Yakima. His name was N. C. (Nick) Richards, and on June 9 he finalized arrangements for the sale of the Yakima Valley Transportation Company to his employer. Yakima Valley Transportation would not lose its corporate identity under the new ownership. The same board of trustees would serve in the new regime. The Yakima Valley Transportation stockholders would be paid off individually by Oregon Railway & Navigation. N. C. Richards would then be installed as Yakima Valley Transportation Company president to enable him to oversee the financial activities of the railroad.

The people of Yakima were not told who had bought their streetcar system. Richards acted publicly as "agent" for the new backers, and he would say only that "in the course of time the people behind this project will be known, and I think that they and their methods of doing business will have the approval of the Yakima public." Robert Strahorn, when the *Herald* alleged him to be the man behind the deal, denied any connection with it. After all, the enterprise was still vulnerable to potential enemies, so why provide any clear targets? The 10,000 shares of Yakima Valley Transportation Company stock were now distributed as follows: 9,997 shares to the Union Pacific, one share to N. C. Richards, one share to F. Hickenbacker, and one share to George W. Beerman.

The effects of the new capital were soon apparent. The North 4th Street project came alive almost immediately. Rails were shipped into town over the Northern Pacific. Two at a time they were hauled by horses from that road's depot to a waiting wagon which carted them to the railhead. The Maple Street line to Sumach Park was begun, and work on the west lines was accelerated. Two additional single-truck cars were ordered from Danville. Orders were placed with the Niles Car Company for an interurban passenger car, a center-cab work motor, and an express freight motor.

Yakima had forever lost its hopes for a locally-owned and locally-operated street railway. The Yakima Valley Transportation Company's franchise had been saved, however, and to its holders would accrue the benefits of big-time railroading and its accompanying wealth. Although Yakimans of 1909 could not foresee it, this outside ownership of their street railroad would become a determining factor in its longevity — a lifespan unequaled by any other electric line in the West.

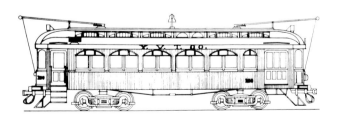

Yakima Valley's interurban cars were big and impressive. In this scene, No. 200 is taking on passengers near Taylor which is in the heart of the farm country north of Selah. The line to Selah and Speyers traversed a variety of scenic changes from city to cliffs and canyons to rolling farmlands. Judging by the car's fresh paint scheme, the photo was probably taken sometime in 1913 or 1914. — KENNETH G. JOHNSEN COLLECTION

6

Interurban Expansion

The influx of Oregon Railway & Navigation Company capital revitalized the Yakima Valley Transportation Company, and between August 1909 and August 1910 the number of its employees tripled. Popular skepticism as to the future of the street railroad all but vanished as one project after another came to life. Completion of the Fairview (fairgrounds) and North 4th Street lines in 1909 made it possible to accelerate work on various other extensions, and the following year saw the greatest expansion in the road's history.

Easter Sunday, March 27, 1910 was the occasion for the opening of the Fruitvale line, running westerly along Fruitvale Boulevard to the north of other routes. The day before, President Richards had made a trial run, proudly announced that all was in readiness, and boasted that the railroad had installed planking on the route out Sixth Avenue that would greatly facilitate crossing of the tracks by wagon teams (not to mention the new-fangled horseless carriages).

What came to be called the Courthouse Loop was now laid around four blocks bounded by Front, B, and Second Streets and Yakima Avenue. Yakima Valley Transportation's company offices stood at First and B Streets, and the loop was intended to form a turning-around point for up-

coming interurban routes. While it was under construction Yakima Avenue was finally double-tracked.

An old 0-4-0 steam locomotive was brought in secondhand from a line in Indiana and used to haul carloads of materials to construction sites and carloads of debris away from them wherever overhead wire had not yet been strung up.

A new joint carbarn and shop facility was erected at Third Avenue and Pine Street. Costing the railroad a whopping $50,000, it was constructed of native stone with a cupola-style wood roof. The main power substation was also built at Third and Pine, and both shop and station are in use today. Within the latter, two large dynamos convert 6,600 volts of alternating current, purchased from Pacific Power & Light Company, to 600 volts of direct current for feeding into the overhead wire.

The longest expansion project of 1910 was the interurban line west to Ahtanum and what was to become Wiley City. The company heralded the convenience afforded the populace of the Ahtanum Valley by this new car service. Soda Springs, a popular tourist spa to the west of Wiley, was now much easier to get to! Patrons could ride the electric cars to the end of the track at Wiley and

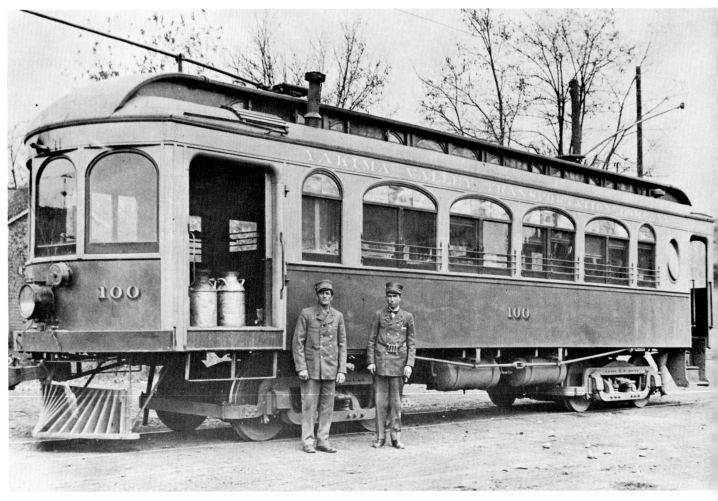

Trainmen portrait with interurban No. 100 in Yakima. Motorman Otto Peske, shown on the left, took part in the ceremonies marking the reinauguration of streetcar service in 1974. — YAKIMA FEDERAL SAVINGS & LOAN ASSOCIATION

After a short career on the YVT during construction, No. 1 went to work on parent North Coast Railway's line as their No. 5 yet still lettered "Yakima Valley Transportation Co." — KENNETH G. JOHNSEN COLLECTION

there switch to pack horses for the trek up to the resort. With the opening up of the Ahtanum Valley, however, vast acreages of cultivated and potential farmland also became instantly accessible by rail. Yakima Valley Transportation's public announcements about the new line failed to mention its private awareness that anticipated freight revenues were the motivating element in completion of the project.

The interurban passenger motor intended for service on the Wiley City run, No. 100, was late in arriving from the builder. The line was ready for opening at the end of May, but no interurban cars were on hand. To institute service the company acquired a couple of knife-edged portholed McKeen gasoline-mechanical cars. These big steel vehicles with their red paint presented quite a contrast to the electric line's diminutive wooden city cars, all of which bore Yakima Valley Transportation's standard yellow and green paint scheme. The McKeens' heavy front power trucks were not suited to a traction line's track and tight radius curves, so they were relegated solely to the new interurban line. Service was begun, with appropriate fanfare, on June 17, 1910 and five daily trips to Wiley City were offered.

For sightseeing tours over its entire system Yakima Valley Transportation ordered a long double-truck car, designated No. 101. Not a typical interurban trolley, No. 101 resembled a strangely overgrown convertible city car. Nevertheless, its attractively appointed oak seats and interior woodwork provided a pleasant traveling environment. The *Seeing Yakima Car*, as it was dubbed, arrived in town during the second week of July, 1910 and made its maiden run, with a carload of company dignitaries and public officials, the evening of July 20. Thereafter it operated on Tuesdays, Thursdays, and Saturdays at 3:30 P.M. and on Sundays at 9:30 A.M. and 3:00 P.M. For 50 cents riders were treated to a three-hour 40-mile round trip over all the lines of the Yakima Valley

Transportation Company. This car was also made available for private charter, and outings on it became a feature of growing up in Yakima. In those halcyon and still almost pre-automobile days it was the *only* way to go.

The line out Summitview Avenue was also pushed to completion in the summer of 1910. Two more single-truck streetcars were purchased for this route, bringing the total number of single-truck cars to seven. Meanwhile, two double-truck city cars had been ordered for service on the city portion of the Ahtanum line, which went out past Johnson's Corners, following a westerly path along the north side of today's Nob Hill Boulevard, to Cemetery Siding (now 24th Avenue). Cemetery Siding was just what its name implied

McKeen gasoline-mechanical rail car No. A-1 and a similar unit were used for a time in 1910 on the YVT's interurban lines before the overhead wire had been completely strung up all the way to Ahtanum and the arrival of the new interurban cars. The McKeens were unable to negotiate the tight curves of the Courthouse Loop, so their use was restricted. Upon arrival of the electric interurbans, the McKeen cars went to work on the North Coast Railway. — YAKIMA VALLEY MUSEUM

35

Straw hats, hoop skirts, an open touring car, and flag-bedecked interurbans signify an important outing — possibly the Fourth of July — circa 1915. Interurban No. 200 is pulling one of the standee trailers along North Sixth Avenue. This is the only known photograph of a standee trailer car in use on the Yakima Valley Transportation Co. — KENNETH G. JOHNSEN COLLECTION

For sightseeing tours over its entire system the Yakima Valley Transportation Co. ordered a double-truck convertible car from the American Car Co., a subsidiary of the J. G. Brill Co., in 1910. The side panels were easily removed to form an open car. Canvas curtains could be pulled down to the floor in case of heavy rain. On arrival the car was dubbed the *Seeing Yakima Car*. — KENNETH G. JOHNSEN COLLECTION

The *Seeing Yakima Car* rolls into Wiley City, circa 1911. The farm houses in this scene stand today, hidden now by trees and other buildings. — BOB LINCE COLLECTION (BELOW) The sightseeing car and interurban No. 100 meet at Ahtanum on a summer's day. Gala excursions in the No. 101 were commonplace in the 1910's and 1920's. This car made a 3-hour sightseeing tour of the entire YVT system for a modest fare of 50 cents. — YAKIMA VALLEY MUSEUM

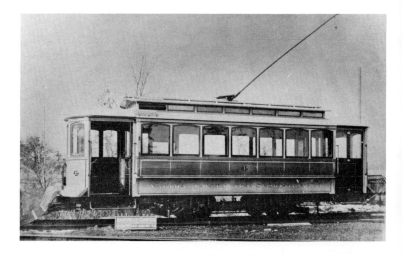

Throughout the history of electric traction the ordinary closed car, either single- or double-truck, was by far the most common type of trolley car. Although the most frequent arrangement for the closed type was with full front and rear platforms, this car was constructed in almost every conceivable arrangement, depending upon the method of fare collection, and whether the car was built for single- or double-end operation. With the completion of the basic system, the Yakima Valley Transportation Co. found itself short of rolling stock in 1910 to handle the increased patronage. The company ordered six new cars, four single-truck trolley and two big double-truck cars. (UPPER RIGHT) Two single-truck cars were ordered from the Danville Car Co. and became Nos. 4 and 5. These cars were from the same builder as Nos. 1-3. —LAWTON GOWEY COLLECTION (RIGHT) Two additional single-truck cars, Nos. 8 and 9 arrived from the American Car Co. — YAKIMA FEDERAL SAVINGS & LOAN COLLECTION (BELOW) Fruitvale Line meets the Selah Line at the corner of Sixth Avenue and Fruitvale Boulevard. Here, single-truck car No. 9 meets a Selah bound interurban. The No. 9 is bound for town and will head out to Maple Street. — BOB LINCE COLLECTION

The 1910 order for new rolling stock included two large double-truck streetcars built by the John Stephenson Co. of Elizabeth, New Jersey. These big cars were 11 feet longer than the single-truck trolleys and had a seating capacity of 36 passengers each. — DUKE – MIDDLETON COLLECTION

Motorman Mark S. Graves and Conductor Pat Potter pose along-side trolley No. 6 in the heyday of YVT passenger service. Note the change in car identification from the above view. An emblem is located in the center of the car, with the numbers now at each end.
— BOB LINCE COLLECTION

In 1914 the YVT supplemented its streetcar fleet with a couple secondhand Stephenson cars from New York State. No. 10 was the former Yonkers Street Railway No. 148 built in 1904. This car was patterned after the Brill semi-convertible design, cars that employed various types of window sash which could either be removed or slipped into the roof or wall pocket during mild weather. The side panels below the windows remained in place. — ROBERT S. WILSON

— a line where the deceased could be transported via interurban to a final resting place in the Yakima Cemetery. Section 9 of Yakima Valley Transportation's Passenger and Freight Tariff stipulated that "a corpse of any person of any age, if accompanied by a person in charge, will be accepted for transportation in the baggage compartment of interurban cars provided person in charge pays the corpse's fare in addition to his own."

The interurban route from Cemetery Siding, after traversing a private right-of-way through Congdon's apple orchards, made an abrupt turn at what became Wide Hollow Junction and proceeded south along what is now 64th Avenue, then west to Ahtanum and Wiley City. A mile or so due west of Wide Hollow Junction, the U.S. Bureau of Reclamation had an irrigation project under construction in connection with which it maintained a large camp near what is today called Westbrook. From Wide Hollow Junction a line was built directly west to serve the camp, and this formed the beginning of what ultimately grew into the Harwood-Henrybro line. Yakima Valley Trans-

portation apparently expected substantial growth in this region, for it quickly purchased two more double-truck cars to serve it. These cars, Nos. 10 and 11, were the only Yakima Valley Transportation cars ever to carry the name of Harwood on their destination sign rolls. In 1926 Wide Hollow Junction became the site of the company's only power substation other than its main plant in Yakima.

Plans for the Maple Street line on the east side of Yakima called for it to cross the Yakima River and proceed eastward to the community of Moxee, and in the fall of 1909, when the Yakima River happened to run unusually low, the railroad hired a contractor to build piers in the middle of the riverbed upon which a bridge could be erected in the future. Only one such pier had been completed before all construction on this line came to a halt, never to be resumed. It had become apparent that Yakima was expanding in a westerly — not an easterly — direction. The bridge pier was removed in 1940. Long before then, however, Moxee (reachable via the Northern Pacific) had given up hope of an electric line from Yakima.

In 1910, as in each of the two preceding years, Yakima Valley Transportation's heaviest volume of passenger business was derived from the annual Washington State Fair. From a firm in Seattle the railroad ordered 12 flatcars upon each of which, at fair time, benches were mounted. There were no walls or roof — just an inward-facing bench on either side of the car and a two-sided center bench. During peak fair hours, to augment the regular service, either the open-deck work car, No. A, or the baggage-express car, No. 300, would pull a string of these specially-equipped flats to the fairgrounds. At the time they represented the ultimate in open-air street railway travel. Today, of course, such an operation would probably never make it past safety codes, environmental impact reports, etc. In 1910, however, little thought was given to any kind of restriction. The company simply went ahead with the innovation regardless of danger from overhead wires. Not until 1914 did it replace the flatcars with four enclosed trailer cars built by the St. Louis Car Company. These trailers were also used for special outings on the Selah line and could be converted to L.C.L. (less-than-carload) freight handling when the need arose.

Ahtanum provided and continues to support the YVT with a substantial freight business. These old flatcars bore the inscription "Seattle Car Manufacturing Co. — Builders." — YAKIMA VALLEY MUSEUM COLLECTION (BELOW) In the early 1910's, before the advent of electric locomotives on the YVT, express motors Nos. 300-301 handled the freight cars. In this scene, No. 300 when new brings four cars of fruit into town from the west Valley along South Nob Hill Boulevard. — PAT POTTER COLLECTION

The convicts that worked at the rock crusher in Selah Gap were housed in this compound. The YVT line is in the foreground and the Northern Pacific line is directly behind the compound. When in use, a high fence and armed guards kept the convicts inside the compound. — BOB LINCE COLLECTION

Selah Valley with the town of Selah in the upper center. The YVT right-of-way is situated along the west side of the road leading into Selah from Yakima. (BELOW) Beautiful downtown Selah in the early 1920's. The YVT tracks cross the road in the foreground. — BOTH BOB LINCE COLLECTION

William Sawyer's hoped-for extension of the Y.V.T. into the lower Valley was one expansion that never came to be. Although he and other ranchers of the region had offered free rights-of-way as early as 1906, the railroad simply had been incapable of growing that rapidly. The picture changed after the North Coast Railway's Y.V.T. takeover in 1909.

Strahorn was building his line up the Valley from the Columbia River. Though labeled the "North Coast Railway" at this time, it was actually no more than an extension of the Oregon Railway & Navigation Company (Union Pacific) into Washington. It passed through Sawyer's territory and eventually ended in Yakima in March of 1911. Yards and shops were constructed in the area between Second Avenue and the Northern Pacific tracks. A direct connection was made with the Y.V.T. in the vicinity of Second Avenue and Walnut Street, thus opening the Y.V.T. to the outside world.

The line to Selah in the north drew perhaps the most enthusiasm both from the railroad and the people it served. Early in 1911 Selah ranchers and farmers held meetings with Yakima Valley Transportation's President Richards and Superintendent Edward M. Kenly and offered to donate the right-of-way, in much the same fashion as ranchers from the lower valleys had done five years earlier. It was not difficult to convince the railroad that abundant business in transporting farm produce lay waiting to be tapped in the territory around Selah. The problem was how to get the railroad from Yakima up through the narrow gap into that community. The Northern Pacific had already taken the best and most nearly level route by laying its tracks on the Selah wagon road and relocating that highway up in the rocks on the side of the gap. Consequently, no room was left for the electric line.

The first solution proposed was to extend the North 4th Street line north and west toward the gap. It would cross the Naches River east of the Northern Pacific crossing, proceed north between the Northern Pacific tracks and the Yakima River, climb up on a viaduct crossing the Northern Pacific tracks and the Selah wagon road, and ultimately drop down into Selah. Subsequent studies showed, however, that the river bottom between the Northern Pacific tracks and the river proper — though it offered the course of least resistance from the center of Yakima — would not provide a sound foundation for the electric railway. Moreover, climbing over the Northern Pacific tracks and the highway and descending from there dictated an excessive amount of elevation change. As a result this plan was scrapped.

The Selah Gap rock crusher in its heyday, about 1912, is shown in the scene at the left. The Northern Pacific tracks are in the foreground. Within another year the YVT tracks would pass beneath the lower building with the gabled roof. — BOB LINCE COLLECTION (RIGHT) Steep cliffs and the concrete foundation of the rock crusher in Selah Gap. — KENNETH G. JOHNSEN

Actual construction of the Selah line did not begin until late 1912. The route Yakima Valley Transportation finally decided upon went north along Sixth Avenue to the west of the Northern Pacific's line, crossed the Naches River just west of the Northern Pacific's crossing, and proceeded along the cliff of the mountain that forms the west side of Selah Gap. Along the sheer embankment it gained altitude, rising considerably above the steam railroad's line.

Taking the westerly route through Selah Gap eliminated the need for crossing the Northern Pacific, the highway, or the Yakima River; but to carve a shelf in the wall of the gap large enough for interurban trains to pass through necessitated extensive excavation. Proximity to the Northern Pacific limited the use of blasting powder, and much of the rock had to be slowly dug away. Whenever powder was used, 24-hour sentinels would be posted along the Northern Pacific tracks below to watch for falling boulders and to stop trains in the event of an obstruction. Great quantities of fill had to be piled into narrow-gauge ore cars and hauled by mule teams from high areas to dumping sites in low ones. Local farmhands were hired as laborers for the magnificent wages of 75 cents per day.

In 1911 a rock quarry and crushing plant had been established on the West wall of Selah Gap to provide gravel for road paving, and Yakima

Electric locomotive No. 298 heads for Selah to pick up refrigerator cars of apples. In this view the locomotive rolls along through Selah Gap. — FRED SCHNEIDER

43

For many years YVT's depot was located at First and B Streets. This was a location inside the so-called courthouse loop from which emanated all of the interurban routes. In this scene, a Jewett built 200 class and the Niles car No. 100 are waiting in the middle of the street in front of the depot. These cars will depart on their respective runs before a city car wants the right-of-way. — KENNETH G. JOHNSEN COLLECTION (LEFT) Motorman Ed Sanders and the No. 200 at Selah about 1918. In addition to commuting passengers, the big wooden interurban cars carried parcels, milk, local and Seattle newspapers, and assorted express from Yakima to the outlying towns. — ROBERT S. WILSON COLLECTION

44

No. 200, one of two large Jewett built combination interurbans, rests quietly in the Washington sun. The motorman aboard these big cars also acted as the express messenger. — LAWTON GOWEY COLLECTION

Valley Transportation's rails eventually passed directly through it. Convicts from the state penitentiary at Walla Walla worked at this quarry and were housed in a compound a little nearer to Selah, between the Northern Pacific's tracks and those of the electric railroad. Although the prisoners have long since departed and the quarry is abandoned, the large concrete foundation of one of the crusher buildings and a natural opening in the rock dubbed "Convict's Cave" are reminders of the activity that once flourished in the area.

The Selah line originally ended at Taylor, but was later extended to Speyer's Station, five or six miles northwest of Selah. The railroad planned to form a loop from there back to Selah, but topography prevented it from doing so. The drop was too steep. Two additional passenger interurban cars and another express freight motor were ordered for use on the new route. The first of these, No. 200, made a trial run over the line on June 21, 1913, providing dignitaries from Yakima, Selah, the Yakima Valley Transportation Company and the North Coast Railway with a gala outing. Motorman for the occasion was Jack Shearer, and the conductor was Pat Potter.

Commanding the attention of one and all on this inaugural trip was old Jack Splawn, by this time mayor of Yakima. As one of the region's pioneers Splawn knew its history like the back of his hand and gave all on board a running commentary about people and events in the districts they passed through. His presence seemed appropriate at the opening of what would be Yakima Valley Transportation's last major expansion. He had guided the traction company through its difficult formative period and now, as it became a truly interurban line, he was undoubtedly proud of his railroad and happy to relax and enjoy its accomplishment.

Freight carloadings were outgrowing the capacity of the express motors as the 1920's arrived. Numerous daily runs had to be made by No. 300. — PAT POTTER COLLECTION

7

Creak Slowly, Old Streetcar

By 1920 the Yakima Valley Transportation Company had reached its maximum size of about 48 track miles. A map of the system in that year reveals clearly the transformation, during its first decade of existence, of what was originally a city transit line into an interurban freight line. All of Yakima Valley Transportation's starter lines, North Fourth Street, North Eighth Street, Fairview, and Maple Street, ostensibly were built for the purpose of carrying passenger traffic. Expansion by means of lines to Selah, Henrybro, and Wiley City, however, tapped freight business. Passenger travel over those routes was merely incidental. To be sure, Yakima Valley Transportation promoted its passenger service, ran the *Seeing Yakima Car,* went all out for fairgoers, and in general gave the impression that its livelihood depended on human riders. Nevertheless, the men in the paneled offices and leather chairs of the Oregon Railway & Navigation Company saw the Yakima Valley Transportation Company as a freight feeder to their steam lines.

Acres and acres of apples had been planted in the fertile land west of Yakima. Packing houses sprang up at Wiley, Ahtanum, Henrybro, Westbrook, and Congdon, as well as at Selah to the north, providing lucrative business for the Yakima Valley Transportation Company.

Lumber soon became Yakima Valley Transportation's second largest source of freight revenue. Cascade Lumber Company's mill on North Eighth Street accounted for many carloads daily. The Cascade mill was served by a Northern Pacific spur, as well as by the electric line. The inevitable competition caused by this situation gave rise to one of Yakima Valley Transportation's unusual traits, a characteristic which as much as any other has been responsible for its longevity — the "personal" quality of its service. Former Superintendent Pat Potter puts it this way:

> I got to be personal friends with the warehouse foreman out at the mill. The U.P. thought I was crazy for even bothering to get to know anyone other than the mill's superintendent or someone else at the front office, but it paid off. Whenever N.P. was late in delivering empty cars to the mill, or even if the lumber to be shipped was situated on the Y.V.T. side of the warehouse, my friend would give me a call and I'd send one of our locomotives out with empties and we'd get the business away from N.P. He'd justify it to his boss by saying he saved them money not having to transfer the lumber clear across the warehouse and leave it waiting for the N.P. cars. And I guess he did in a way.

47

This imposing villa was built by apple magnate Chester Congdon and has become legendary in the Yakima Valley. Congdon had become wealthy in the East through his iron and steel holdings. He moved to the Valley and purchased huge tracts of fertile orchard land and constructed the castle. He did not live to enjoy it, however. His descendents now use it as a summer home. The grounds were not completed when this photograph was made in 1915. Today the grounds surrounding the castle are lush and gardenlike. The stone waiting station along the track still stands today, although it is no longer used. The Congdon Orchards are still the largest single block of apples in Yakima, and the warehouse in the distance still ships many carloads of Washington Delicious apples every year. — WRAY BROWN COLLECTION

One of the big interurban cars rushes by the Congdon castle en route to Wiley. The YVT line cuts right through the Congdon property. So important was Congdon that he rated two stops on the line: One the small station near the castle, and the freight stop known as "Congdon." — WRAY BROWN COLLECTION

Yakima Valley Transportation established the same rapport with its fruit-packing customers. At some of the Selah warehouses the road again competed with the Northern Pacific, and former Motorman Walt Shoot recalls:

> The packers didn't like the Northern Pacific. They weren't flexible. N.P. crews would have to ask the packers for free apples and if they were lucky, they'd get one or two reject apples. We were always patient with the packers. If it took longer than planned to load the cars, we'd wait for them. And we'd never charge them to switch cars the way N.P. would. When we finished our day at the warehouses, we'd often find three boxes full of red delicious apples on our footboards (one for each crew member) as we departed.

The alliances it made with these influential customers helped see the Yakima Valley Transportation Company through franchise problems in later years.

When Walter S. Howard of Spokane became Yakima Valley Transportation's superintendent in 1920 he upgraded freight service with the purchase, secondhand, of the road's first truly freight-only locomotive, No. 299. The company published freight tariffs like those of major na-

Express motor No. 301 has just pulled into the YVT yard in Yakima on Pine Street. Judging by the flatcar it is pulling, it was probably out performing maintenance work on the line. No. 3 and electric locomotive No. 299 are also seen in this 1920 scene. — LAWTON GOWEY COLLECTION (BELOW) The YVT purchased this second-hand locomotive in 1920 to handle the increased freight traffic. The engine was built for the United Railways of Oregon, and was sold to the Oregon Electric Railway before coming to the YVT. — DONALD DUKE

Electric locomotive No. 297 easily handles 9 empty refrigerator cars along Nob Hill Boulevard. No. 297 was acquired in 1942 from the Union Pacific which used it for switching in Glendale, California. — WILL WHITTAKER (OPPOSITE PAGE) Express motor No. 300 continued to handle freight cars when required.

This box motor was not powerful enough to handle more than four loaded freight cars at once. — PAT POTTER COLLECTION Yakima Valley Transportation Co. Time Table No. 14 included both city street car schedules and the interurban lines. — KENNETH G. JOHNSEN COLLECTION

tional railroads, since it connected with the latter via the Union Pacific's Oregon Railway & Navigation Company. However, instead of listing major cities or commerce centers as its stations the way large railroads did, Yakima Valley Transportation had to content itself with enumerating its streetcar and interurban stops. Thus, in theory at least, a dealer back East could get a tariff and ship freight directly to destinations such as South Nob Hill Boulevard, Washington or Naches River Bridge, Washington.

By 1920 there was little doubt in anyone's mind that Yakima Valley Transportation was seriously into the freight business. Concurrently Yakima was undergoing a phenomenon that was occurring all across the country with startling speed. Private automobiles were changing America's transportation picture. The State Fair continued to provide the railroad with a healthy patronage during the last week in September. *Seeing Yakima* specials and evening *Moonlight Rides* to an amusement park called The Hippodrome sporadically boosted ridership totals. But overall passenger business, particularly on the East side, was declining. Conversion of Yakima Valley Transportation streetcars to one-man operation and reduced headway provided some relief;

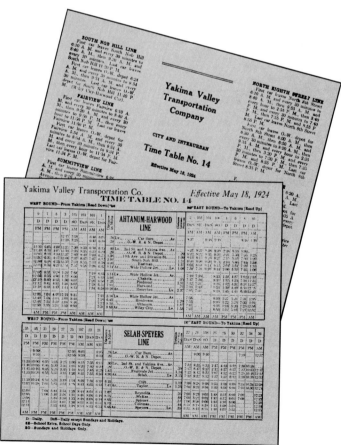

Interurban No. 100, at Henrybro, circa 1920. The little waiting depot at the right was typical of the shelters built at most of YVT's rural interurban stops. — KENNETH G. JOHNSEN COLLECTION

Outfitted with a tower and other contraptions for maintenance purposes in 1922, Niles motor No. A became the YVT's mainstay for line work. In this view, No. A scoots along Yakima Avenue near the Northern Pacific crossing. — ROBERT S. WILSON

but the inexorable advance of the automobile came on.

Several armed holdups had taken place at the end of the North 4th Street line, in a decaying part of town, and in 1921 the railroad decided to abandon it. Also abandoned were most of the Maple Street line and that part of the Fairview line extending beyond the fairgrounds. All planned passenger line extensions were written off. One of these was a line long-awaited by residents of the Broadway district. In earlier days the railroad had been so certain it would extend in this direction that orders for several of its streetcars included Broadway among the specified destinations on their sign rolls. Broadway was one destination these cars would never reach.

Private jitney operators appeared on the scene and eroded Yakima Valley Transportation's passenger traffic even more. An over-confident one predicted he would put the streetcars out of business within five years. The traction company, however, beat him at his own game. In 1924 it obtained the city's permission to replace the Summitview streetcar with a bus. The latter, a Mack bus, No. B-1, proved instantly popular, and Yakima Valley Transportation rented a second from Seattle to handle the overflow. Two more Mack buses were purchased in 1925 for use on the same line and also to augment streetcar service on the Fairview line during fair week.

In 1926 Yakima Valley Transportation petitioned the city to allow it to replace all of its streetcars with buses. The city refused. The intent of the grantors of the franchise 20 years earlier had been that the road should provide rail passenger service wherever it handled freight. To give in to its request would be, in effect, to abandon the purpose of the franchise — rail transit service — and to provide Yakima Valley Transportation, i.e., the Oregon Railway & Navigation Company, with a complex freight-only feeder on the streets of the city.

The Yakima city fathers did allow the railroad to experiment with bus service on some lines, and not all instances were as successful as the Summitview replacement. Ridership on the Fruitvale-North Eighth Street route, for example, actually declined to such an extent that trolleys were restored after a few dismal months. In spite of this, in 1929, Yakima Valley Transportation presented another bus substitution petition to the municipal powers. Shortly thereafter it received another denial.

In the face of what was becoming a hopeless situation the railroad launched one final effort to make trolleys profitable again. In August 1929, much to the surprise of nearly all Yakimans, the

electric line ordered three brand new streetcars of the very latest design from the American Car Company (Brill). Called *Master Units* by Brill, these streamlined all-metal cars were slightly ahead of the much-heralded PCC cars which came into use in various parts of the country seven or eight years later. Yet their modern features made them much closer kin to the PCC's than to the wooden deck-roof trolleys that had been plying the streets of Yakima since 1907. The interiors of the new cars were well-lighted and boasted plush leather seats and smooth composition floors. Yakimans anticipated their arrival with almost as much excitement and enthusiasm as they had the delivery of the first trolleys over 20 years before.

On February 28, 1930 the first two *Master Units* arrived in Yakima on flatcars, covered with tarps imprinted American Car Company. (The third would arrive a week later.) They were at once rolled into the shops — flatcars, tarps, and all — and curious onlookers got not so much as a peek at them. Nevertheless, the sleek lines under the tarps confirmed their radically new design. Robert S. Wilson, Yakima's lifelong Y.V.T. observer-enthusiast, noted in his daily diary of Yakima Valley

While brand spanking new, *Master Unit* No. 21 was displayed to an admiring public at the Union Pacific-Yakima Valley Transportation Co. depot on Second Avenue — Saturday March 8, 1930. — ROBERT S. WILSON

Master Unit No. 20 on a training run in March 1930. The car made repeated runs over the various lines to acquaint motormen with the new equipment. — ROBERT S. WILSON

53

Interior view of car No. 22, one of the new *Master Units*. Leather seats, composition floor, and abundant lighting made these new trolleys much more popular than the old wooden cars. These cars were designed for one-man operation when built. The fare collector was located next to the motorman. — LAWTON GOWEY

Yakima Valley No. 22 is about to cross the Northern Pacific tracks on Yakima Avenue. The Holtzinger Building in the background still stands today, the Northern Pacific tracks are still in operation, but it is now Burlington Northern. The only thing missing today is the trolley and the tracks on Yakima Avenue. — ROBERT S. WILSON

Three scenes at the YVT shops. (RIGHT) Interurban No. 100 basks in the sun outside the shop building in the early 1930's. (LOWER RIGHT) The carbarn with locomotive No. 298, a *Master Unit,* and line car A. The building was built in 1910 along with the shops next door. (BELOW) Car No. 5 outside the shops. — ALL ROBERT S. WILSON

Transportation doings: ". . . the shape of the new cars is very different from the old ones, the new cars being longer and much lower." In color, too, they departed from the norm — at that time standard Pullman green. These cars were light green, decorated with two shades of blue, and finished off with yellow striping!

Unloaded and untarped on Saturday, March 1, the *Master Units* made Yakima Valley Transportation's other vehicles appear all the more ancient, and a sad but realistic Wilson penned the following tribute to the old wooden trolleys whose days were now obviously numbered:

> Creak slowly, old streetcar, along thy last line!
> Thy roof, it is leaky; and torn is thy sign.
> A new car stands ready to run in thy stead,
> So get thee right back to thy own old car shed.
>
> Thou old thing whose rattling resounds through the town,
> Thy fender is drooping; thy trolleys are down.
> When you go back to the barn, you must go to the back
> And take up thy place on an old junkyard track.
>
> How lofty, old streetcar, you looked when you passed,
> In the days when we thought your speed really quite fast.
> But now that the new cars have come here to stay,
> There's nothing for you but, "Get out of the way!"
>
> How pleasant it was in those days long ago,
> When out to the fairgrounds or down to the show,
> We rode, on thy seats which today seem so queer,
> Which induce some to laugh and most others to jeer.

> Thy motors are old and thy wheels turn slow,
> But still on thy run thou hast been wont to go,
> Through many long years, thou most faithful have been,
> But now your time's done and they're turning you in.
>
> Creak slowly, old streetcar, along thy last run!
> Tomorrow in the new cars we'll ride just for fun.
> But still we'll remember those days now soon past
> And regret in some ways that you're running your last.
>
> —With apologies to Burns

Sure enough, upon the arrival of the *Master Units* all of Yakima Valley Transportation's single-truck cars were retired. Two of them had been freshly repainted for the 1929 fair season, but even they were no longer needed. No. 5 made the final single-truck car trip on March 5, 1930 along the Fruitvale-North Eighth Street route. But for Robert Wilson's daily notebook the event would have passed unnoticed into history. Big Interurban No. 101, which had made its last run the year before, was also retired at this time. Within three months every single-truck car — and No. 101 as well — had been mercilessly burned and its scrap metal remains hauled off in gondolas.

The city routes were now left with seven double-truck cars: the four older wooden cars — Nos. 6, 7, 10, and 11; and the three new Brills — Nos. 20, 21, and 22. For these seven, and indeed for Yakima Valley Transportation's entire passenger traffic operation, it was do or die. There were no other alternatives.

The introduction of the new Brill built *Master Unit* streetcars to Yakima in 1930 brought about a new renaissance in passenger travel on the YVT. In this scene, No. 22 glides along Yakima Avenue en route to Fruitvale. — WILLIAM C. JANSSEN

8
Interurban Decline

The introduction of the *Master Units* to Yakima brought about a mild renaissance in streetcar patronage. Children enjoyed riding to and from school on the modern cars, although "bobbing" them was impossible ("Bobbing" was a prank of the 1920's wherein a group of schoolboys stood together on a trolley's rear vestibule and jumped up and down in rhythm with the single-truck car's bobbing until they bounced it off the track!) Housewives could now go shopping in relative comfort regardless of the weather, and old-timers no longer had to climb perilously high steps to get aboard. Fate, however, in the form of the unrelenting onslaught of the personal automobile, with its privacy and unrestricted freedom of destination and timing, was not about to let the streetcars regain all they had lost.

Interurban traffic was now declining more rapidly than city traffic. The convenience of the automobile had replaced the elegance of traveling from Selah to Yakima and Wiley City on the stately wooden interurban cars. Bob Lince, Selah's most knowledgeable historian, remembers riding the interurbans as a boy, dreaming the while that he was really a rich mustachioed businessman with a big black stogie riding in his private railroad palace car. The baggage compartments of the interurbans carried everything from the mundane to the other worldly, from newspapers and milk cans to the somber casket of someone recently departed. In summer Lince would get off the car before it reached downtown Selah, thereby saving five cents of the money his mother had given him for trolley fare, which he would then use to purchase one large ice cream cone at the corner drugstore. The ice cream was consumed before he reached home, and his mother was never the wiser!

By the early 1930's, in the midst of Depression era reality, the interurban passenger operation was losing big money for the Yakima Valley Transportation Company. Some days there would be only bundles of the *Portland Oregonian* and the *Yakima Daily Republic* keeping the motorman company on the trek to Wiley and Selah. Even though motormen and conductors were paid only 50 cents an hour at the time, the cost of providing the service greatly outran the income it generated. As a first step toward greater economy, the big interurban car on the Selah run was replaced with a city car, usually No. 7, equipped for one-man operation. Dark and creaky, old No. 7, with its

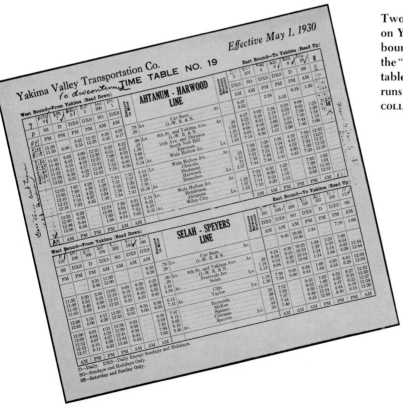

Two *Master Units* pause in front of the Baptist Church on Yakima Avenue to pick up churchgoers. No. 21 is bound for "South Nob Hill" and No. 22 is scheduled for the "Fruitvale" Line. — WILLIAM C. JANSSEN On his time table at the left, Bob Wilson noted all the discontinued runs on this interurban schedule dated May 1, 1930. — COLLECTION OF KENNETH G. JOHNSEN

longitudinal wooden bench seats, hardly improved the popularity of the run and patronage continued to decline.

Nick Richards, having guided the growth of Yakima Valley Transportation since 1909, retired in late 1933. His successor, A. A. Murphy, sought to bring passenger losses under control. As of that year the State Fair was no longer being held, and some drastic cutbacks in passenger service were being proposed. In 1934 Yakima Valley Transportation filed to abandon all interurban passenger service, but requested that it be allowed to continue freight business over the interurban lines. The railroad argued that the city could not tie permission to continue hauling freight on the lines in question to continued carrying of passengers because the Yakima city council did not hold jurisdiction over lines connecting other towns. Selah immediately countered the railroad's petition with a request that Yakima Valley Transportation be required to add a noon run to Selah because there was not enough service as it was!

At this point the county commissioners agreed to hold a hearing on the matter. This meeting, which took place December 20, 1934, was well-attended by farmers from far and near. Some spirited discussion took place, but silence reigned after one of the commissioners took a poll that revealed only two people had ridden to the hearing by rail! The commissioners then recommended

Fruitvale bound trolley rolls along East Yakima Ave. between Naches and Sixth Streets. — ROBERT S. WILSON (BELOW) With the decline in express and all kinds of freight chores, No. 301 was relegated to track maintenance service. — CHARLES SMALLWOOD

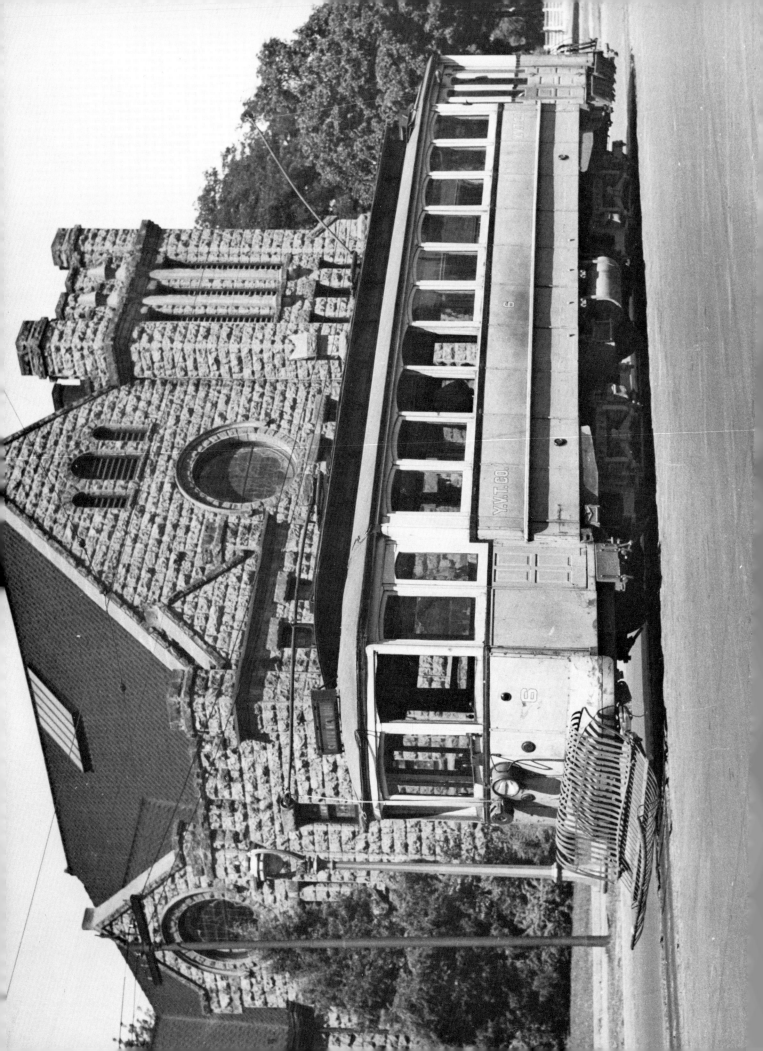

Yakima Valley Transportation Co. No. 22 waits at Fruit-vale Road and Powerhouse Road, terminus of the Fruit-vale Line. The motorman has reversed trolley poles, but has yet to turn the seats. — WILLIAM C. JANSSEN (OPPOSITE PAGE) A warm July day in 1946 finds No. 6 wearily trudging west on Yakima Avenue. The still standing Baptist Church in the background was built the same year that YVT laid its tracks on Yakima Avenue. — LAWTON GOWEY (RIGHT) Time table No. 22 issued during the depression is somewhat spartan and the form printed on a mimeograph machine. — KENNETH G. JOHNSEN COLLECTION

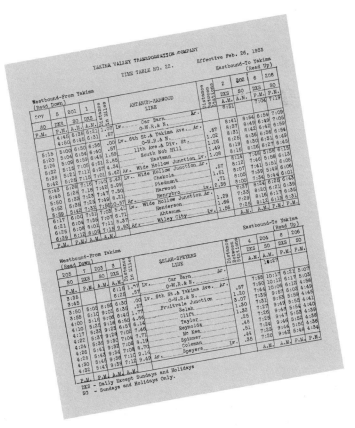

In the above scene, trolley No. 6 grinds along Sixth Avenue bound for Fruitvale. (LEFT) Rail photographer Al Farrow pointed his camera out his hotel window one day in the early 1940's just in time to catch *Master Unit* No. 22 going by. While Yakimans enjoyed the show at the Roxy, Farrow would rather watch the parade of street-cars. — BOTH AL FARROW (LOWER LEFT) Trolley No. 22 crosses the Northern Pacific tracks past the depot, circa 1940. — STEVE MAGUIRE COLLECTION

that Yakima Valley Transportation be allowed to suspend interurban passenger operations. They acknowledged, however, that final approval of the suspension would have to come from the State Supervisor of Transportation in Olympia. It was received the following April, and final runs were scheduled for May 15, 1935. J. Wallace Estes, who had come to the Yakima Valley from Spokane with Walter Howard, was motorman for the last trips. They were made without fanfare, and as the final car pulled in at 7:10 P.M. the only people aboard were Motorman Estes and enthusiast Robert S. Wilson.

In June 1938 Yakima Valley Transportation abandoned and tore up its Fairview line. Loss of the State Fair had made this line unnecessary from the standpoint of either passengers or freight. Cars Nos. 10 and 11 were scrapped and their carcasses hauled down to the Union Pacific yards where they served as tenements for a time.

In April 1940 the Twin Coach Company demonstrated a couple of its buses in Yakima. Compared to the old Macks the big Twin Coaches were supremely modernistic. Management and motormen alike were impressed, and orders were placed for two 23-seat models. In an effort to improve ridership Yakima Valley Transportation also modernized streetcar No. 6. In place of its longitudinal benches it received transverse seats from the scrapped interurban cars. An attractive gray-green-cream color scheme which had been

During those World War II years, the Christmas decorations were not the same without the colored lights. In this early 1940's scene on Yakima Avenue, trolley No. 22 passes the old Hotel Washington, a familiar landmark in many of the early Yakima illustrations. — KENNETH G. JOHNSEN COLLECTION

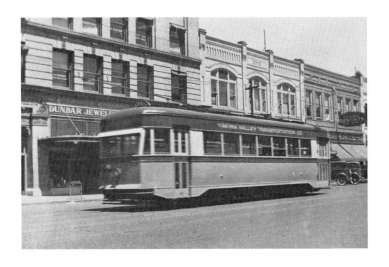

A sleek, newly painted *Master Unit* hurries past the Miller Building in 1936, location of Yakima's leading physicians and dentists. — ROBERT S. WILSON (BELOW) Trolley No. 22 has just crossed 6th Avenue and takes off for South Nob Hill. Traffic is quite light on this crystal clear afternoon. — AL FARROW

applied to the *Master Units* in 1935 was now applied to No. 6 as well. Although the changes were refreshing, the modern steel buses were still more appealing to John Q. Public, and in 1942 two more Twin Coaches were ordered.

Greater numbers of autos on the roads meant increased chances of their colliding with rail-confined trolleys. There were smash-ups. The *Master Units* had scarcely entered service when their sides and door glass panels began to show the scars of altercations with private vehicles. The death toll from trolley-auto accidents grew, and the trolleys' popularity declined in proportion. Although most of the accidents were caused by poor judgment on the part of the automobile drivers, Yakima's public officials began to criti-cize the Yakima Valley Transportation Company's motormen.

Such criticisms were for the most part un-deserved. There were a few "bad apples" in the barrel, though, such as the motorman on No. 21 who one evening was rounding Johnson's Corner outbound onto Nob Hill from 16th. The route here

Streetcars frequently stood unoccupied on Pine Street during layovers while their motorman sauntered over to the carbarn to pick up orders, eat lunch, or chat with the boys. — WILLIAM C. JANSSEN

climbs a hill going west. At a yard part way up the hill a drunken driver had earlier crashed through a picket fence bordering the electric line, leaving debris scattered over the track. As No. 21 passed the spot part of the wrecked fence knocked off the petcock from its air reservoir, leaving it without air for its brakes. When he saw the air pressure gauge drop to zero the motorman panicked. Instead of calmly driving the streetcar to the top of the hill and rolling to a stop, he ran back through the car shouting, "Everyone jump off! We have no brakes!" The less-than-brave chap then proceeded to become the first one off the car.

Trolley No. 21 started rolling backwards down Nob Hill toward 16th as the last of the passengers jumped off. It gained momentum, careened around Johnson's Corner at a high rate of speed, and zoomed along 16th Avenue heading back into Yakima. Its trolley pole was still set for the opposite direction, and sparks flew and wires

snapped as it snagged the overhead along the car's wild flight. Miraculously, the trolley did not collide with oncoming traffic. Superintendent Potter lived on 16th Avenue, and he just happened to be coming home from work at the time. He glanced at No. 21 heading toward him and realized that something was wrong. Jumping out of his car (yes, even he drove an automobile to work), he ran down the street toward the trolley. As it neared him he reversed direction and ran back, letting the speeding car catch up with him. As it passed he jumped on, and as smoothly as the hero in any western movie reversed the controller and brought the errant car to a stop. "That motorman had the audacity to come to me the next day and ask if he still had his job," Potter recalls.

In October 1946 the 40-year franchise granted to the Yakima Valley Transportation Company in 1906 expired. In negotiating its renewal the city hoped to incorporate some very specific desires

With the congested street traffic of Yakima Avenue left behind, trolley No. 20 glides toward its terminus on North Eighth Street. A small boy leans toward the open window to experience the breeze. (BELOW) Old No. 6 passes the Fruit Exchange Building on Yakima Avenue as it rolls east to North Eighth Street. — BOTH AL FARROW

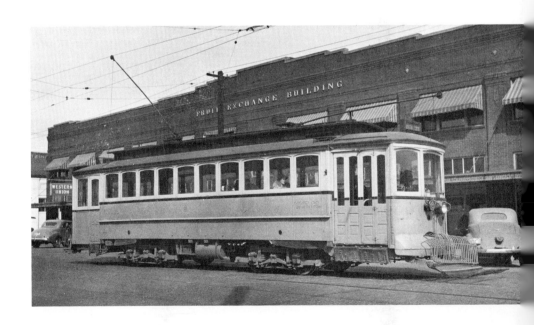

into the new document. Post-World War II automobile density had turned Yakima Avenue into an extremely busy thoroughfare, and the city no longer wanted Yakima Valley Transportation tracks taking up the middle of it. The council pointed to declining trolley ridership and the popularity of the modern buses and said, in effect, "We want to get the tracks off Yakima Avenue." Now the Yakima Valley Transportation Company would have loved to convert from trolley to bus, not only on Yakima Avenue but on all of its other lines as well. To remove the tracks from the Avenue, however, would be to lose freight access to the east side and in particular to the Cascade Lumber Company mill. Parent Union Pacific did not wish to part company with such a valued customer. Therefore, in a complete reversal of previous positions, Yakima Valley Transportation now proposed, in exchange for renewal of the franchise without amendments, to modernize its streetcar fleet with PCC cars and to upgrade its passenger service!

The city remained adamant. The tracks on Yakima Avenue had to go. Rail-weary auto-loving citizens voiced opposition to franchise renewal and demanded that any such renewal be limited to a period of not more than ten years. Seeing that Yakima Avenue was pretty much lost, Yakima Valley Transportation worked out a compromise with the council. It agreed to give up the Avenue and all trackage on the east side of Yakima if, in return, it could suspend *all* passenger service but continue to maintain its west side lines for freight and connections with its tracks to Wiley, Henrybro, and Selah. The company also pushed the franchise duration to 25 years.

Although the electric railroad thus agreed to a major amputation, it was at last able to throw off the cloak (perhaps yoke is the better word) of passenger business and function openly and entirely as the freight feeder to the Union Pacific that it essentially had been since 1909. For their part the people of Yakima, in their desire to be rid of the clattering old trolleys (theirs was the only city in the state where trolleys still operated), compromised the intent of their original franchise and allowed a freight-only railroad to operate on some of their streets.

Only the sound of the air compressor informs a passing motorist that No. 301 is a working train in maintenance service. The crew are taking a noon day lunch break and snooze. — WILL WHITTAKER

9

At Low Ebb

During the weeks immediately preceding its final streetcar runs, Yakima Valley Transportation was plagued by troubles of a mechanical nature. A broken axle on No. 6, broken rail joints, and a number of accidents kept repair crews busy and made everyone increasingly eager for it all to come to an end. The last trips were scheduled for February 1, 1947. To mark the occasion a "Parade of Progress" began at 7:00 P.M. that evening with Streetcar No. 7, carrying the Davis High School Band, in the lead. A warm *Chinook* wind had melted the usual February snow, and the balmy air brought out plenty of spectators. Through the trolley's open windows the crowds could hear the band playing as the procession made its way down Yakima Avenue from Sixth Street on the east side to Sixth Avenue on the west. Trolley No. 7 was followed by the *Master Units,* Nos. 20, 21, and 22. Then came the original hood-type Mack buses, and after them no fewer than 12 Twin Coaches. Several of the latter had just arrived in Yakima, and since there were not enough motormen and bus drivers to go around, Superintendent Potter had had to persuade the Twin Coach sales representative to operate one of them.

When the parade reached the finish line on Sixth Avenue, old No. 7 trundled off to the carbarns. The *Master Units* and buses, however, continued operating over their regular runs until the usual 12:00 A.M. quitting time. For the rest of the evening the streetcars were rather heavily patronized by Yakimans wanting one last ride; but the prevailing mood was more one of good riddance than fond farewell. Operating the last car to roll into the yards that night was J. Wallace Estes, the only motorman who had not elected to be retrained for bus operations. When the trolleys retired, so did he.

The remaining wooden cars, Nos. 6 and 7, were soon scrapped. The once proud *Master Units* encountered a happier fate, however. Eventually sold to the Portland (Oregon) Traction Company, the trio put in another ten years of service on that line. Then, in the early 1960's, they were purchased by members of the Puget Sound Railway Historical Association for their museum near Snoqualmie Falls and thus returned to Washington State.

Yakima Valley Transportation continued to operate Yakima's buses, for in addition to the

A warm Chinook wind melted the February snow and brought out a sizable crowd for the "Parade of Progress" down Yakima Avenue. Riding the Hyster and "Rising with Yakima" were members of the Chamber of Commerce who had come to applaud the cessation of streetcar service. — KENNETH G. JOHNSEN COLLECTION (BELOW) No. 21 on its last day of operation in Yakima, February 1, 1947. — AL FARROW

amended railroad franchise it had received a separate ten-year bus franchise. When this expired in March of 1957 the company decided not to renew it, since use of the buses — like use of public transportation all across the country — had steadily declined during the decade. A private firm took over the franchise, but soon went broke. Thereafter the city itself began operating bus service and as of this writing it is still doing so.

Rails were removed from Yakima Avenue — and from most other non-used routes — in the summer of 1947. Some sections were simply paved over. With the loss of east side freight service electric locomotives Nos. 299 and 300 were withdrawn and retired from service. They were scrapped in the mid-1950's. Nos. 297 and 301 were retained, as was the venerable No. 298, but the railroad reduced the number of its operating crews to two and ultimately to only one. Locomotive No. 298 continued in active service, while the harder-to-switch No. 297 became a standby.

Although carloadings of freight now amounted to no more than 2,500 to 3,000 annually, the style of Yakima Valley Transportation freight service did not change. Conductor Walt Shoot and his crew perpetuated the personal good feelings between railroad and shipper. Moreover, while some adults along Nob Hill Boulevard may have cursed the railroad, scores of boys and girls along that thoroughfare and also 16th, Pine, and Sixth Avenue came to recognize Walt's friendly grin and Mel Lucas' waving hand. When apples were in season, the men would often toss a few out to their youthful fans.

Used and unwanted: streetcars and buses no longer needed by the YVT await their fate at the company yard in 1947. — LAWTON GOWEY

With the last trips completed on February 1, 1947, the wooden rolling stock was soon scrapped. The *Master Units* encountered a happier fate and eventually were sold to the Portland Traction Company, Portland, Oregon, and the three cars saw another 10 years service on the Oregon City and Bell Rose Lines. In the view above, former YVT No. 21 as Portland Traction No. 4009 is in the Portland yards. — BOB GRAY

Portland Traction No. 4010, former YVT No. 22, rolls through Ardgour stop en route to Oregon City in 1948. — CHARLES D. SAVAGE (RIGHT) Two of YVT's *Master Units* as they look today as preserved by the Puget Sound Railway Historical Association at their museum in Snoqualmie, Washington. The two cars are Nos. 20 and 21. —KENNETH G. JOHNSEN

Trolley Signals

Many of the nation's interurban lines operated without any automatic signals and chose to run by time table and/or train orders. Interurbans which chose a signal system had many types of oddball equipment to select from. The YVT chose this interesting block signal system, shown at the left. A car entering the block trips a wire causing the semaphore arm to go down. A car approaching in the same direction, seeing the arm down, knows that a car is ahead in the same direction. The second car proceeds with caution. At the other end of the block a semaphore facing the other way goes horizontal showing a car is approaching. The car approaching a full block must take a side track until the car in the block passes by. If there are no cars in the block, the arm rests halfway between vertical and horizontal. Today this system is inoperative as the YVT uses two-way radio. — HARRE DEMORO AND KENNETH G. JOHNSEN

The backbone of any railroad system is its shop facilities. A single trolley out of service for any period of time could badly disrupt the scheduling of service. The YVT built its trolley barn and shops out of stone in 1910 at 3rd Avenue and Pine Street. (LEFT) A peek inside the shops where most of the machinery was belt driven. (BELOW) Yard end of the wooden trolley barn and shops. The barn was torn down in 1976, but shops are still used. Work too big is sent to the Union Pacific shops in Oregon, Idaho, or Wyoming. — BOTH KENNETH G. JOHNSEN

Map of the yard layout, shops, and substation. The building in the lower right is the new Yakima Interurban Trolley Lines storage facility. (BELOW) GMC buses for the city system continued to be serviced in the YVT shops until the early 1970's. The bus service facility was moved a few blocks away and the old trolley barn torn down. — BOTH KENNETH G. JOHNSEN

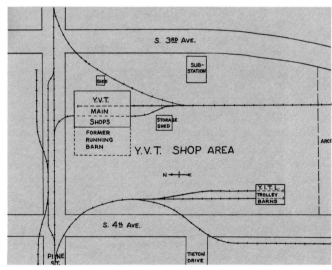

Old Shops

With the resumption of trolley service in Yakima, a new facility was required to keep the two cars under cover when not in use. The new structure is found in the lower right hand corner of the map on the opposite page and in the lower left hand corner of the aerial photograph shown below. — FREDERICK A. JOHNSEN (LEFT) Electrical work that can't be performed at YVT's shops is sent out to firms such as General Electric, whose Kent, Washington shops overhauled trolleys Nos. 1776 and 1976 in 1978.

Substation

The YVT substation is located in the Yakima yard and shop facility. Here 6,600 volts of Alternating Current commercial power are received from the power company and converted to 600 volts of Direct Current for use in the overhead wires. The substation consists of transformers to adjust the power company voltage to the input current of the motor-generator sets of the substation. These motor-generators are nothing more than an AC motor driving a smaller DC generator to line voltage. (ABOVE) The main YVT substation. A booster station is located at Wide Hollow Junction to maintain line voltage on the Wiley and Henrybro Lines. — KENNETH G. JOHNSEN (LEFT) The electric panel and one of the motor-generator sets. — HARRE DEMORO (LOWER LEFT) The two motor-generators in the substation. — KENNETH G. JOHNSEN All power is turned off when the electric locomotives or the YITL cars are not in use.

Headquarters

The Union Pacific office building located at 104 West Yakima Avenue, is home to the Yakima Valley Transportation Company. From his corner room (shaded by the lowered awning) YVT Manager Jerry Price directs the affairs of the electric railroad. This structure is also the Union Pacific district freight offices, office of the Union Pacific Fruit Express and the UP credit union. The balance of the building is the Union Pacific's L.C.L. freight terminal and team tracks. — KENNETH G. JOHNSEN

YVT's electric locomotives were originally painted black. To make the locomotives more visible to the ever increasing numbers of automobiles on Yakima streets, a brighter color scheme evolved. In the 1950's and 1960's the locomotives were Armour yellow with silver and black trim. In 1970 they were painted in the standard Union Pacific yellow, gray, red, and silver dress which they wear today. Flashers on rooftop and ends are an even more recent addition. (ABOVE) No. 298 in black livery. — WILL WHITTAKER (BELOW) No. 298 as it appears today. — KENNETH G. JOHNSEN

Collisions between Yakima Valley Transportation locomotives and private autos continued to be a problem. In an effort to make the former more visible the railroad changed the color of Nos. 297 and 298 from somber black to bright yellow with silver and black trim. Not until 1970 were they painted in the standard Union Pacific color scheme of yellow, gray, and red. To further increase the engines' visual impact reflectorized stripes and lettering and roof-top flashers were added.

Despite such safety measures in the public interest, the railroad's popularity was by 1971 at low ebb. Yakimans remained frustrated by the anachronistic tracks in their streets and that year, as the expiration date of Yakima Valley Transportation's 25-year franchise approached, they began objecting to them even more vociferously than they had in 1946. By campaigning solely on an anti-Yakima Valley Transportation platform one politician even talked his way into a seat on the city council. "Safe Streets Committees" sprang up and their activist members began circulating petitions among the voters asking the city to refuse to renew the agreement — or at least to put the question of renewal to a vote of the people. The council, however, realized that under the terms of the city's charter the latter action would be illegal.

Over six miles of YVT tracks traverse Yakima city streets and run along the side of the road in two locations against the flow of car traffic. — FRED SCHNEIDER AND KENNETH G. JOHNSEN (BELOW) Turning onto Sixth Avenue from Pine Street, No. 298 heads for Selah in 1971. — KENNETH G. JOHNSEN

Freight Service

In its infancy, YVT freight service consisted of boxes, barrels, flats, and other parcels of less-than-carload size shipments piled aboard express motor No. 300 and carried into town for transfer to Northern Pacific trains. Connection, in the Spring of 1911, with the North Coast Railway brought into being YVT's role as a freight feeder and interchange with cars from all over the country.

A refrigerator car icing facility was erected beside a long spur track in the North Coast (Union Pacific) yards near the YVT connection. The track was equipped with overhead wires so that YVT's electric locomotives could switch cars on it. Packing houses sprang up along lines in all the fruit growing districts. Indeed, at the terminus of each interurban line was a fruit packing warehouse.

Although the YVT has always been closely associated with the hauling of apples, pears, and other luscious produce of the valley, it has also counted lumber as one of its most basic staples.

Packing house fires, competition from trucking, and relocation of businesses farther out in the country are threatening to further erode YVT's base of freight operations. Remaining customers, however, are fiercely loyal and appreciate the personal, however-you'd-like-it style of service provided by the yellow electric trains.

On the opposite page, a sight that is very commonplace to most Yakimans, but long forgotten elsewhere is an electric locomotive trundling down the middle of the street with a few cars in tow. — KENNETH G. JOHNSEN (BELOW) No. 298 switching the Union Pacific interchange tracks near the YVT's own yard. — FRED SCHNEIDER

West Pine to Wide Hollow

The freight lines to Wiley and Henrybro, running west from Yakima, run in city streets a portion of the way. (LEFT) Sitting on the window sill gives motorman John Kilsimer a better view as he switches the spur tracks on West Pine Street. — HARRE DEMORO (BELOW) Waiting patiently for its crew who are inside the barn, No. 298 and its train presents an obstacle to Pine Street motorists who should be used to such operations. Some people, unfriendly toward the railway, object to driving around the locomotive and cars, are trying to get the electric trains off Yakima's streets forever. — KENNETH G. JOHNSEN

Electric traction motors grind as No. 298 rolls slowly along West Pine Street with a single boxcar in tow. — FRED SCHNEIDER (BELOW) Nob Hill motorists must yield to YVT's No. 297 as it leaves the protection of the private right-of-way and enters the traffic pattern on one of Yakima's busier thoroughfares to the west. — KENNETH G. JOHNSEN

Rolling along Nob Hill Boulevard in the afternoon sun's waning light, half-century-old No. 298 and a couple reefers head for Westbrook. (UPPER RIGHT) Apple blossom time in the Yakima Valley. The air in the orchards at this time of year is unbelievably fragrant. In this scene, No. 298 rolls through the heart of Congdon's orchard with the castle in the background. — BOTH KENNETH G. JOHNSEN

Wiley and Henrybro Lines

Interurban lines were extended west into the Ahtanum Valley in 1910. With the opening up of this new territory, vast acreages were placed into cultivation, especially red Delicious apples. The original passenger routes to Wiley City and Henrybro soon developed into heavy seasonal freight branches as mouth-watering fruit was loaded and shipped to all corners of the nation. In the scene at the right, Clasen apples are being loaded into a Union Pacific Fruit Express car. Note the carton reads "The World's Finest Apples." (BELOW) In about five months the delicate off-pink blossoms become red Delicious apples. Trees become so heavily laden that they are propped up with boards to keep the branches from breaking. — BOTH KENNETH G. JOHNSEN

Spring's winds are rapidly changing the skies west of Yakima as Yakima Valley Transportation Co. No. 298 brings a loaded refrigerator car of apples in for interchange. Soon a light April shower will dampen the ground and bead up on the road's well burnished rails. — KENNETH G. JOHNSEN

Wide Hollow Junction in the 1940's. The straight track takes off for Henrybro, with the Wiley City section curving to the left. — KENNETH G. JOHNSEN COLLECTION· (RIGHT) End of track at Wiley City. — KENNETH G. JOHNSEN

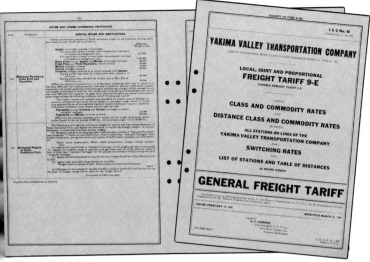

Selah Line

A new interurban line was extended north of Yakima to Selah via Selah Gap in 1912-1913. The Selah Line originally ended at Taylor, but was later extended to Speyer's Station, several miles northwest of Selah. The region surrounding Selah was fast becoming a rich agricultural region and provided the YVT with additional freight revenues. At the left, a copy of the YVT tariff providing all rates for shippers. (CENTER LEFT) No. 298 switching at Yakima Pine Products. (OPPOSITE PAGE) A short train headed for Selah moves along North 6th Avenue of Yakima — BOTH FRED SCHNEIDER (BELOW) In the mid-1950's, No. 298 rumbles along North 6th Avenue after crossing the Northern Pacific (now Burlington Northern) tracks. — CHARLES SMALLWOOD

The route to Selah crosses the Naches River over this two span curved cord Through Truss Bridge. The spot is a favorite for floaters, skinny-dippers, and fishermen. — WILL WHITTAKER

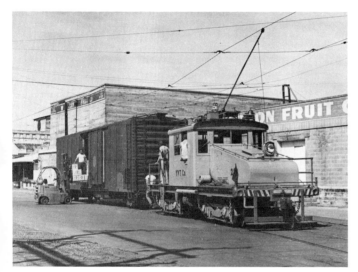

The curves are so tight on the wye track at Selah, that even short-wheelbased No. 298 squeels loudly as it rounds the curve. Trackage such as this is one reason diesels have not taken over from the nimble-footed electrics. — KENNETH G. JOHNSEN (LEFT-CENTER) Electric locomotive No. 298 patiently hums away while warehousemen load a refrigerator car with a load of Larson apples at Selah. — FRED SCHNEIDER (BELOW) Yes, it snows in Yakima, even though the Chamber of Commerce states the region has 300 annual days of sunshine. It is seldom that snow keeps the trains from running. In this scene, No. 297 handles four cars of freight along Sixth Avenue, bound for Selah. — JOHN L. AINSWORTH

Steep cliffs and narrow right-of-way are a part of the scene as the Yakima Valley road's Selah Line climbs through Selah Gap. In the above view, locomotive No. 298 and two cars roll through the Gap en route to Yakima. The Burlington Northern tracks are on the right. — FRED SCHNEIDIER

In the face of so much public clamor, parent Union Pacific's lawyers for the Yakima Valley Transportation Company remained cool, resorting to the somewhat oblique tactic of insisting that inasmuch as the freight railroad's existence was governed by the Interstate Commerce Commission, the city really did not possess the final say-so in the matter. Hemming and hawing on the part of both parties to the franchise lasted for about 13 months, during which time the railroad operated for one year on a temporary franchise extension and for one month on no franchise at all!

In the end Yakima Valley Transportation received a good deal less than it had requested. Franchise duration was reduced once again, this time to ten years, and numerous requirements as to safety, warning appliances, and even hours of operation were included. Should future franchise renewals follow the pattern of 1946 and 1971, the embattled Yakima Valley Transportation Company may well expire altogether before the end of the 1980's.

Form definitely did not precede function when the design for line car No. A was made. Gaudily clattering down Sixth Avenue, it is almost enough to make one laugh at the car with its tower, ladders, and various kinds of wire hanging from loops and reels from every corner. For railroaders, however, the humor is tempered by the appreciation of the fact that this genuine 1910-vintage antique serves a purpose. Few pieces of interurban rolling stock are in active service that are quite as old as the venerable Number A. (CENTER LEFT) Linemen work on a trolley hanger on the Nob Hill line relocation in 1973. — BOTH JOHN L. AINSWORTH (LOWER LEFT) Heading west through blooming orchards near Westbrook, No. 298 passed Bob Jones and the line car who have yielded the main line to the outbound freight. — KENNETH G. JOHNSEN COLLECTION

The Line Car

Rails wear out with traffic or rust out with disuse. Ties decay, or are worn by the base of the rails, or are rendered useless by too-frequent driving of spike-holes which become too many and too large. Ballast disappears into the mud beneath, and mud appears in the ballast above. Bolts loosen and joints sag. Ditches fill up and drainage becomes clogged — or, rather, all these and countless other results of deterioration and decay come about unless there is constant vigilance and care, the endless cycle of work known as track maintenance. In the scene below, the track crew installs new ballasted rail on a curve, complete with guard rail. — WILL WHITTAKER

Track Maintenance

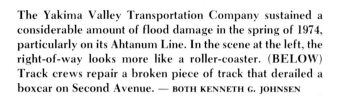

The Yakima Valley Transportation Company sustained a considerable amount of flood damage in the spring of 1974, particularly on its Ahtanum Line. In the scene at the left, the right-of-way looks more like a roller-coaster. (BELOW) Track crews repair a broken piece of track that derailed a boxcar on Second Avenue. — BOTH KENNETH G. JOHNSEN

While the track crew are supposed to maintain track, they also have to pull 'em up at times. In the above view, the crew pulls out the rails on Yakima Avenue in 1947. — AL FARROW (RIGHT) YVT's single-point switch guides the train's wheels from the "back" side of the flange instead of in the conventional way. — BOTH KENNETH G. JOHNSEN

It is October 12, 1974, the day of the streetcars' inaugural public runs. Union Pacific President John Kennefick was guest of honor at the inaugural ceremonies and piloted the first car out. Bunting-draped, flag-bedecked No. 1976 is seen here on one of its first public runs that day, entering the private right-of-way that cuts through Congdon's orchards. — KENNETH G. JOHNSEN

10

Streetcar Renaissance

From 1947 on, at least once or twice in every decade, the idea of reviving streetcar service over Yakima Valley Transportation Company tracks was dug out of the back closet and dusted off. The company itself never fostered the idea, of course, because passenger hauling was clearly a losing proposition, and in a deficit-ridden age of increasing government regulation what railroad is going to espouse an unprofitable operation if it does not have to? As the 1970's dawned, however, Walt Shoot and others in the Yakima Valley Transportation work force confided to the author of this volume that they thought bringing streetcar rides back to Yakima might engender in the public mind some good feeling toward the railroad. They all agreed, though, that such an operation would have to be self-supporting or publicly subsidized because in no way would management take on that kind of financial burden.

The owner of two of the former Yakima Valley Transportation *Master Units* was enthusiastic about returning them to Yakima for renewed use — if not for regular transit service, then at least for a tourist-oriented operation. He told this author he felt sure that a scheme could be worked out for

maintenance and operation of the cars in Yakima, if someone would underwrite the cost of transporting them from the museum in Snoqualmie. The ingredients were all there: streetcars, electric railroad, willing personnel, and the need for service. What was lacking was a catalyst to fuse them into some workable form.

In February 1973 the author presented to the Yakima city council a summary of these ingredients and the possibilities inherent in them. One councilman, a grocery store chain owner by the name of Wray Brown, was impressed. Brown was a man with friends in high places both locally and in the state capitol. A superb politician, he was not only a "doer," but an excellent judge of character, and he also admitted to a latent interest in streetcars and cable cars that went back many years.

Wray Brown wholeheartedly adopted the streetcar revival idea, for he realized that Yakima Valley Transportation's recent franchise ordeal had not only tarnished the railroad's public relations, but hurt the city council's image, too. A pleasant old-fashioned streetcar ride as a source of public enjoyment might detract from the un-

95

A YVT *Master Unit* sits derelict in the forest behind the Puget Sound Railway Historical Association Museum at Snoqualmie, Washington. Ferns, vines, trees, and rot from the heavy rains that fall on this area are taking their toll. — KENNETH G. JOHNSEN (BELOW) STCP shops in Oporto, Portugal, where Yakima's two new streetcars were refurbished. The running gear of soon-to-be No. 1776 is standing between the rows of parked wheels. — PAUL CLASS

pleasantness of the contested franchise.

A number of seemingly enormous problems manifested themselves immediately: Permission from the railroad would be needed to reinstate streetcar service on the trolley tracks. An independent organization and source of funds must be set up to render the operation financially self-sufficient. The streetcars would have to be brought to Yakima, made safe and operable, and decently housed.

Predictably, Yakima Valley Transportation and Union Pacific management were frankly unsympathetic to Brown's request for permission to operate streetcars on their rails. The councilman pressed his mission all the way to the top of the parent company, however, and contacted Union Pacific President John Kennefick himself. To bolster Brown's credibility Washington's Governor Dan Evans also sent a plea to President Kennefick, whose reaction was one of complete support. The good word filtered down through management echelons like magic.

Brown then formed the Trolley Advisory Committee, composed of a number of prominent Yakimans who not only supported the trolley idea, but were in a position to help bring it to life. Several influential fruit shippers, happy to be of assistance in something that might guarantee the road's continued operation, pledged substantial sums. Shades of 1906 and the Commercial Club! Moreover, since the nation's Bicentennial Cele-

STCP No. 261, an identical twin to Yakima's Nos. 1776 and 1976, was one of several trolleys inspected by Paul Class for possible purchase by Yakima. No. 261 continues in routine operation in Oporto, Portugal, to this day, unaware of the fame growing around its two sisters in faraway Yakima. — PAUL CLASS

bration was only three years away, American cities were already being encouraged to set up heritage-related programs to tie in with the national observance. The Yakima streetcar project was a "natural" for this purpose, and Brown successfully petitioned the federal government for official Bicentennial Project status (and funds).

An inspection trip to Snoqualmie, made by the untiring councilman in company with several Yakima Valley Transportation Company personnel, revealed that to bring the *Master Units* up to par would require a great deal of work. Moreover, Brown felt that Yakima should own any cars it operated, and in their case that would not be possible. Thus a search for streetcars began, in the course of which this writer contacted or visited over 20 trolley museums throughout the United

States. Paul Class, the tall Lincolnesque curator of the Oregon Electric Railway Association's museum at Glenwod, Oregon, was certain he could obtain some very old wooden Brill cars, closely resembling Yakima's early wooden trolleys, in Europe. They would even be fully operable, since they were still in use on the streets of Oporto, Portugal.

Delighted with this possibility, Brown decided to send the curator on a fact-finding trip to Portugal in October-November of 1973. Class carried with him on the journey a personal letter from the mayor of Yakima to the Mayor of Oporto asking to buy two of his city's streetcars. Arrangements were worked out whereby Yakima purchased two wooden single-truck cars for 90,000 *escudos* ($3,150) each, along with 100,000 *escudos*

In the view at the left, Portuguese streetcar craftsmen work on the future No. 1976's truck in the shops in Oporto. Yakima's cars were assembled in these shops in 1927 from parts supplied by the J. G. Brill Company. (RIGHT) The rebuilt truck that will soon ride under Yakima Interurban Trolley Lines No. 1776 awaits mating to its carbody in the spring of 1974. — BOTH PAUL CLASS

worth of spare parts. Under Class' personal direction the trolleys were refurbished and repainted in Oporto.

By that time one year had turned into the next, and Portugal — in the spring and summer of 1974 — was in the throes of revolution. All contact with the Portuguese involved in the streetcar transaction was lost soon after the cars were delivered to the docks in Oporto for shipment to the United States. All that was certain was that for the duration of the conflict freighters were not docking at Portuguese ports. At best it was probably going to be a long wait.

In the interim, however, Brown and his committee did not lack for alternative concerns: How were the streetcars to be transported from a United States port overland to Yakima? Would their tires be wide enough, or would the trolley cars just drop between the Yakima Valley Transportation Company's sometimes erratic rails? Would inflation devalue the dollar, ballooning 90,000 *escudos* into an impossible figure? Would vandals destroy the trolleys between port and Yakima? The worrying went on, to such a point that Brown's favorite observation became, "On the day that I, Wray Brown, can walk up and kick one of the tires, then on that day I will be a Believer!"

The uncertainties about shipping ended when Yakima received a letter from the port of Houston, Texas advising that streetcars had arrived for Yakima and requesting payment for shipping and handling. Brown sent Class to Texas, where the

Gleaming with fresh paint, soon-to-be YITL No. 1776 is ready to leave STCP shops for the dock at Oporto, Portugal. — WRAY BROWN COLLECTION

(LEFT) On the docks at Houston, Texas. It had been the plan to ship the trolleys to a West Coast port such as Seattle or Vancouver. — WRAY BROWN COLLECTION (CENTER) "When I, Wray Brown, can walk up and kick one of their tires, then on that day I will be a Believer!" He became a believer on August 28, 1974. (RIGHT) On August 28, 1974, the trolleys arrive in Yakima. — BOTH KENNETH G. JOHNSEN

latter got the trolleys loaded onto flatcars and safely on their way to Washington State. They arrived in Yakima in the very early morning hours of August 28, 1974, and history began to repeat itself. Just as it had celebrated the coming of Yakima Valley Transportation's new beauties 67 years before, Yakima now declared a holiday in honor of the arrival of these "new" trolleys — an occasion replete with speeches and a public display of the bright red and white cars. Wray Brown did not fail to ceremoniously kick one of their tires.

On August 29 both cars were unloaded onto Union Pacific rails, towed over to Yakima Valley Transportation's connection, and pulled onto the electric line's tracks. Paul Class raised the trolley pole on No. 1776, ending a 27-year absence of streetcars, and ran the car up Pine Street to the Yakima Valley Transportation Company's yard. This writer then ran it into the yard, whereupon all four wheels promptly left the gravel-covered rails. As Yakima Valley Transportation crews worked for an hour with jacks and a tow truck trying to re-rail No. 1776, Class took No. 1976 on its first run up to the carbarns.

In the above view, the streetcars move to the YVT interchange. (BELOW LEFT) Paul Class raises trolley pole to the wire for the first time. (BELOW RIGHT) Oops! Shallow flanges and gravel covered rails lifted the trolley off the rails. — ALL KENNETH G. JOHNSEN

No. 1976 is unloaded from its flatcar in the Union Pacific yard and pushed to the YVT by a UP truck with rail wheels. — KENNETH G. JOHNSEN

Work must go on for the YVT freight crew, even though the new streetcars are giving Yakimans a new thrill this Columbus Day, 1974. The No. 1976 has taken the siding at Congdon's warehouse to let the No. 298 and its single car train pass. Mel Lucas waves out of the steeple cab at the new trolley's enthusiastic passengers. — KENNETH G. JOHNSEN

After the derailment the first day the trolleys arrived, the cars were placed in the YVT shops to have their tires widened and flanges ground deeper. — LAWTON GOWEY

No. 1776 was eventually hauled back on the track and bedded down inside Yakima Valley Transportation's shops. Breathing a sigh of relief Brown, Class, the Union Pacific and Yakima Valley Transportation crews, and this correspondent all piled onto No. 1976 for a gala ride up Pine Street, Tieton Drive, over to 16th Avenue, and return. Yakima finally had its trolleys!

In the course of the next seven weeks motormen were trained, wheel flanges were ground deeper, and preparations for public operations began. Retired firefighter Ben Alaimo was hired as trainmaster, and motormen were recruited from off-duty firefighters. Although they had offered to take part, Yakima Valley Transportation Company personnel were not included in the planning or operation, and it was left to big Ben to learn the ropes on his own.

(LEFT) The author at the controls of No. 1976. — LAURI JOHNSEN (CENTER) Wray Brown, successful Yakima grocer and politician, guided the Yakima Interurban Trolley Lines through its formation and helped to bring to life the dream of renewed trolley service on Yakima Streets. (RIGHT) The new Yakima trolleys on their first day of service in the pastoral farmlands west of Yakima. — BOTH KENNETH G. JOHNSEN

Columbus Day, 1974, or Christmas Day, 1907? There was not a heck of a lot of difference between the two. Public speechmaking, followed by gala first runs in wooden single-truck streetcars marked both days in Yakima, Washington. The cars in this photograph are passing Wide Hollow Junction in the heart of the apple country. — KENNETH G. JOHNSEN

Streetcars began running down the middle of Yakima streets in 1907 and in 1979 they're still at it. Not the same ones of course, but the single-truck wooden car shown here on Pine Street is a close kin to that which opened YVT service. (RIGHT) In the spring of 1975, a man, his wife, and infant child came all the way from Erie, Pa. to rent this trolley. The car is shown approaching Henrybro on the extreme western terminus of the road. — **BOTH KENNETH G. JOHNSEN**

Trolley No. 1976 rolls along Nob Hill Boulevard en route to the western end of the line. (BELOW) The same car in the apple orchards, with Golden Delicious apples on the trees and a few on the ground. — BOTH KENNETH G. JOHNSEN

Wiley City on a charter in 1976. Charters have become a popular way for schools, churches, and clubs to have a weekend outing and relive the days of their youth. — KENNETH G. JOHNSEN

Yakima Valley Interurban Lines motorman's hat was patterned after an old time passenger trainman's cap. (UPPER RIGHT) Trolley No. 1976 stands on Pine Street in front of the YVT shops like a ghost from the past. (BELOW) The Burlington Northern (formerly Northern Pacific) and the Yakima Valley Transportation Company lines come together at the Naches River and parallel each other through Selah Gap. The BN takes the lower route along the path of the old Yakima-Selah wagon road. — ALL KENNETH G. JOHNSEN

Little has changed in the panorama on the left during the last sixty years. The highway is the major difference. The view is looking north from Selah Gap toward the town of Selah. The concrete abutment on the left is all that remains of the rock crushing plant that once flourished here. Above it on the hillside can still be seen a remnant of the relocated Yakima-Selah wagon road. (ABOVE) Like a ghost from the past, car No. 1776's lights illuminate the right-of-way as dusk comes to Selah Gap. Yakima's streetcars keep the wires singing on weeknights in the summer. (BELOW) The Northern Pacific took the easy way through the Gap. Latecomer YVT had to carve a route in the cliffs above. Running along the cliff makes for a thrilling trolley ride. — ALL KENNETH G. JOHNSEN

To reach Selah, the YVT has to cross a Burlington Northern branch on Sixth Avenue in Yakima. This is today the only crossover on all of the YVT's 21 miles of line. Trolleys are required to stop, check for BN trains, give two blasts on their air horns, and proceed. — KENNETH G. JOHNSEN

Trolley No. 1976, and No. 1776 a short distance behind, have rolled down Selah Gap and are entering the town of Selah. — KENNETH G. JOHNSEN

Maintaining a pool of competent motormen proved difficult at first. Some of the firemen were excellent at the job, handling it with the same expertise and professionalism that they brought to their firefighting duties; but others were genuinely not interested in the streetcars and soon dropped out. Eventually, however, people from other walks of life entered the pool: a school principal and his wife, an engineer, orchardists, students, a college instructor, a dentist, a Union Pacific official and his son. To provide narration during the public trips a group of hostesses called "The Trolley Dollies" was formed. Public operation began with a christening ceremony on Columbus Day, 1974, highlighted by the appearance of Union Pacific President Kennefick, as well as three retired Yakima Valley Transportation streetcar motormen: Pat Potter, Elmer Evans, and the late Otto Peske.

With each succeeding year of operation ridership of the trolleys has continued to grow, and in spite of the rampant inflation of the 1970's the Yakima Interurban Trolley Lines (as the operation calls itself) is holding its own. It boasts two handsome antique trolleys, a carbarn, and a van and trailer — all fully paid for!

Whether the trolleys will successfully achieve the original goal of restoring the Yakima Valley Transportation Company to public favor before the time for its next franchise renewal rolls around remains to be seen. At the very least, however, Yakima's sources of civic pride have been notably enhanced by its possession of two of the finest examples of the early American streetcar operating on what is probably this country's best-preserved authentic electric railroad, Washington's apple country interurban.

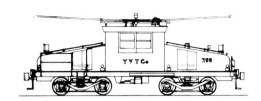
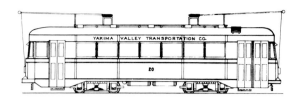

Appendix

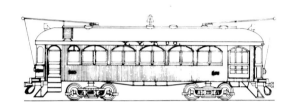

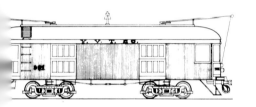

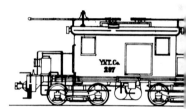

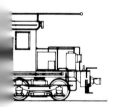
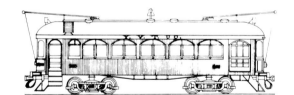
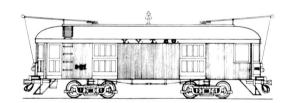

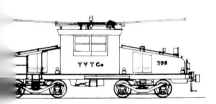
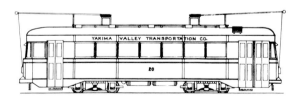
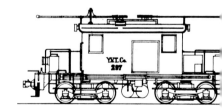

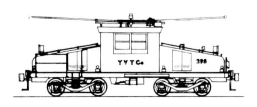
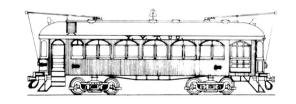

Roster of Rolling Stock

CITY STREETCARS

Car No.	Type	Builder and Date Built	Total Length*	Seats	Trucks	Traction Motors	Controls*	Remarks
1	Closed	Danville - 1908	29'6"	20L	ST/Brill 21-E	2/General Electric 80	K-9	Scrapped 11-12-1926
2	Closed	Danville - 1908	29'6"	20L	ST/Brill 21-E	2/General Electric 80	K-9	Scrapped 11-12-1926
3	Closed	Danville - 1908	29'6"	20L	ST/Brill 21-E	2/General Electric 80	K-9	Outfitted for welding work in 1922. Scrapped 6-4-1930
4	Closed	Danville - 1910	30'11"	24L	ST/Brill 21-E	2/General Electric 80	K-9	Scrapped 6-4-1930
5	Closed	Danville - 1910	30'11"	24L	ST/Brill 21-E	2/General Electric 80	K-9	Scrapped 6-4-1930
6	Closed	Stephenson - 1910	42'	8L 28T	DT/Brill 27-G	2/General Electric 80	K-9	Converted to 34 seat (longitudinal) in 1918. Returned to 36 seat in 1938. Scrapped in 1947
7	Closed	Stephenson - 1910	42'	8L 28T	DT/Brill 27-G	2/General Electric 80	K-9	Converted to 34 seat (longitudinal) in 1918. Scrapped in 1947
8	Closed	American - 1910	32'6"	24L	ST/Brill 21-E	2/General Electric 80	K-9	Scrapped 6-4-1930
9	Closed	American - 1910	32'6"	24L	ST/Brill 21-E	2/General Electric 80	K-9	Scrapped 6-4-1930
10	Closed	Stephenson - 1904	39'5"	16L 24T	DT/Brill 27-F	4/General Electric 80	K-28-B	Former Yonkers Ry No. 148. Purchased in 1914. Scrapped 9-27-1939
11	Closed	Stephenson - 1904	39'5"	16L 24T	DT/Brill 27-F	4/General Electric 80	K-28-B	Former Yonkers Ry No. 149. Purchased in 1914. Wrecked and received vestibule from No. 9 in 1929. Scrapped 10-10-1939
18	Closed	Brill	29'6"	20L	ST/Brill 21-E	2/General Electric 80	K-9	Rented from Tacoma Ry & Power as their No. 18 to open service. Operated December 1907 - October 1908
20	Closed	Brill - 1930	40'10"	12L 28T	DT/Brill 177-EIX	4/Westinghouse 510-E	K-75	Sold to Portland Traction as their No. 4008 in 1948. At Puget Sound Railway Hist. Assn. Museum at Snoqualmie, Washington.
21	Closed	Brill - 1930	40'10"	12L 28T	DT/Brill 177-EIX	4/Westinghouse 510-E	K-75	Same PT No. 4009
22	Closed	Brill - 1930	40'10"	12L 28T	DT/Brill 177-EIX	4/Westinghouse 510-E	K-75	Same PT No. 4010
36	Closed	Brill	29'6"	20L	ST/Brill 21-E	2/General Electric 80	K-9	Rented from Tacoma Ry & Power as their No. 36 to open service. Operated December 1907 - October 1908
1776	Closed	Brill - 1927	32'6"	8L 24T	ST/Brill 21-E	2/Italian General Electric	B-54-E	Built by STCP in Oporto, Portugal from Brill parts. Owned by City of Yakima
1976	Closed	Brill - 1927	32'6"	8L 24T	ST/Brill 21-E	2/Italian General Electric	B-54-E	Built by STCP in Oporto, Portugal from Brill parts. Owned by County of Yakima

*Controls and the total length of cars in some cases represents the author's studied estimation, owing to the lack of complete information in the company's official records.

L — Longitudinal Seating
T — Transverse Seating
ST — Single Truck
DT— Double Truck

INTERURBAN PASSENGER / EXPRESS CARS

Car No.	Type	Builder and Date Built	Total Length*	Seats	Trucks	Traction Motors	Controls*	Remarks
100	Combine	Niles - 1909	45'	2L 36T	Standard C-50	4/General Electric 80A	K-28-F	Retired to maintenance service. Scrapped 1947.
101	Convertible	American - 1910	43'	52T	Brill 27-G-1	4/Brill E-1	—	Scrapped 6-4-1930
200	Combine	Jewett - 1913	45'2"	2L 36T	Brill 27	4/General Electric 80	C-97-A	Scrapped 10-13-1939
201	Combine	Jewett - 1913	45'2"	2L 36T	Brill 27	4/General Electric 80	C-97-A	Scrapped 10-12-1939
300	Express	Niles - 1909	44'10"		Standard C-50	4/General Electric 80A	K-28-F	Scrapped 1956
301	Express	Jewett - 1913	45'		Brill 27	4/General Electric 80A	C-97-A	Sold 11-71 to California Ry. Museum for parts. Dismantled by early 1972.

L — Longitudinal Seating
T — Transverse Seating

*The total length of cars and the controls in some cases represents the author's studied estimation, owing to the lack of complete information in the company's official records.

ELECTRIC LOCOMOTIVES

Car No.	Type	Builder and Date Built	Total Length		Trucks	Traction Motors	Controls	Remarks
297	Switcher	Baldwin/ Westinghouse - 1923	32'		Baldwin	4/Westinghouse 562D5	HLF-9	Note A
298	Switcher	General Electric - 1922	34'		Alco RM63B	4/General Electric 207-2	MC90A	Note B
299	Switcher	Baldwin/ Westinghouse - 1907	30'		Baldwin	4/Westinghouse 83	L-3	Note C

Note A: 50-ton steel cab switcher built as Glendale & Montrose No. 22. Became Union Pacific E-100 during May 1931. Purchased by YVT in March 1942. Presently in standby service. Builder's No. 56937.

Note B: 50-ton steel cab switcher built for the YVT. Presently in service. Builder's No. 8788.

Note C: 35-ton steel cab switcher built as United Railway of Oregon No. 1. Became Oregon Electric No. 15. Purchased by YVT in 1920. Scrapped in 1958. Builder's No. 32061.

MAINTENANCE EQUIPMENT

Car No.	Type	Builder and Date Built	Total Length		Trucks	Traction Motors	Controls	Remarks
A	Line Car	Niles - 1909	40'		Standard C-50	4/General Electric 80-A	K-28-F	Originally a flatbed car with center cab. Outfitted in 1922.

MISCELLANEOUS EQUIPMENT

1   An 0-4-0 steam locomotive purchased secondhand, reportedly from the Terre Haute & Indianapolis Railroad. Used for construction of track where overhead wire had not yet been installed. Became North Coast Railway No. 5 about 1910 and was used in that road's construction. About 1922 sold to a local logging road and subsequently scrapped.

A-1   A diesel weed burning machine was used by the YVT in the 1930's and 1940's. Disposition is unknown.

A-1   A McKeen gasoline-mechanical car was built for the Yakima Valley Transportation Co. in 1910, but lettered for the North Coast Railway as North Coast A-1. Along with another North Coast McKeen car it provided interurban service on the Wiley City line until the arrival of Yakima Valley Transportation's electric interurban cars. The McKeens then went into service on the North Coast Railway between Yakima and lower valley towns. They carried 65 passengers, baggage, and express freight and were capable of 60 m.p.h. speeds.

51-54   The YVT purchased four arch-roofed passenger trailers from the St. Louis Car Co. in 1915 to handle overflow crowds during State Fair season, as well as for special excursions. The seats were removable, allowing use of the trailers for Less-than-Carload freight or greater passenger capacity (150 standees). They were sold to Teanaway Logging Co. in the early 1920's, where they were used to haul lumberjacks into the woods. The cars were later scrapped.

1014   A flatcar with boom, presently in maintenance service.

1015   Flatcar, presently in maintenance service.

——   Twelve flatcars were constructed in Seattle for the YVT in 1910. Several were outfitted with benches to haul additional passengers to and from the State Fair in open-air comfort.

——   A homemade double-truck tower trailer was used for line work prior to 1922. At this time No. A was equipped with a tower. Prior to construction of the tower trailer, a tower was mounted temporarily on rented streetcar No. 18.

——   In May 1935 a wooden streetcar body from Seattle was obtained and stripped of its vestibules, mounted on maintenance bogie, and pulled by a horse up and down Yakima Avenue during Frontier Days. It holds the distinction of being the only horsecar ever to operate in Yakima.

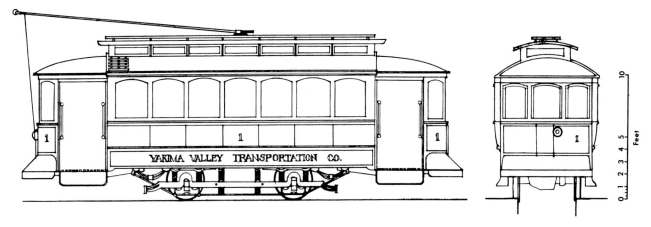

City Cars Nos. 1 - 5

Although double-truck street railway equipment came into use during the early 1890's, many new systems unsure of potential patronage purchased stock cars from builders. On a single-truck car the weight of the carbody was carried to the truck frame by means of coil springs, usually located at either side of the axles, and by elliptical springs mounted on extensions of the truck frame. Because of the short wheelbase, single-truck cars had a tendency to pitch and to "nose" from side to side. As a result they were not smooth riding. (LEFT) Builder's photo of Yakima No. 3. Nos. 1 to 3 were identical. — KENNETH G. JOHNSEN COLLECTION (BELOW) A busy day in Yakima in 1908. The lone Danville-built car coming from the west appears to have no traffic problems. — YAKIMA VALLEY MUSEUM COLLECTION

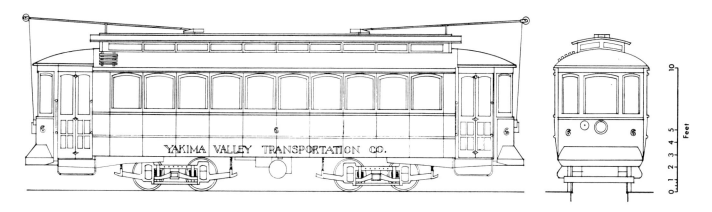

YAKIMA VALLEY TRANSPORTATION CO.

City Cars Nos. 6 - 7

Shortly after the turn of the century, carbuilders began to use greater amounts of steel in carbody construction. The most common arrangement of double-truck cars was a full front and rear platform design. Passengers could load from the rear and leave from the front. (LEFT) Interior of car No. 6. The car was built with transverse seats, replaced by longitudinal benches in 1918, and changed back in 1938. — LAWTON GOWEY (BELOW) Car No. 6 on beside-the-road trackage. — WILL WHITTAKER

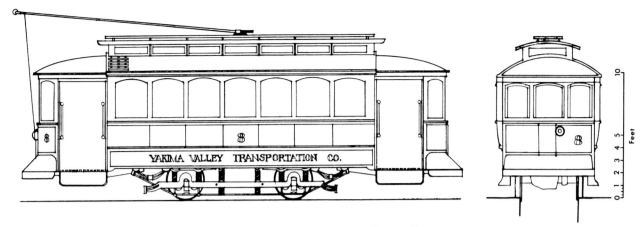

City Cars Nos. 8 - 9

The Yakima Valley purchased two additional single-truck cars in 1910 for light traffic lines. Cars Nos. 8 and 9 were identical to the other single-truckers except in car length. (LEFT) Builder's view of YVT No. 8 at the American Car Co. plant in St. Louis. — EDWARD B. WATSON COLLECTION

The motorman and conductor pose for the camera out on the line. The motorman is dressed in a racy pin-striped suit, while the conductor has on the typical Yakima Valley Transportation frock coat. Note the carnation in the lapel! — KENNETH G. JOHNSEN COLLECTION

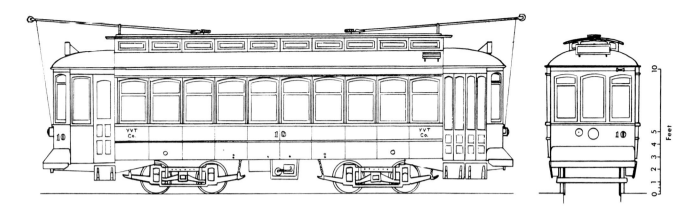

City Cars Nos. 10 - 11

The road purchased two secondhand double-truck cars from the Yonkers Railway in 1914 to supplement the basic service. These cars had a larger platform on each end, but only a single door at the rear. — VINCENT F. SEYFRIED, FROM JEFFREY WINSLOW

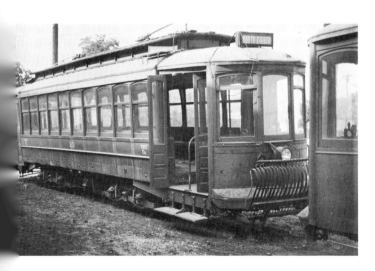

The former Yonkers cars, built in 1904, were withdrawn from service prior to World War II. (ABOVE) No. 10 out of service. — ROBERT S. WILSON (LEFT) Another view of No. 10 in the Yakima yard ready for the scrapper. — CHARLES SMALLWOOD

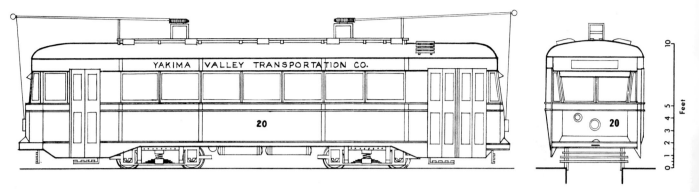

City Cars Nos. 20 - 22

Three new trolleys of radical design were purchased from Brill in 1930. The cars were very swift and smooth riding, thus patronage picked up immediately. (LEFT) Builder's view of No. 20. — LAWTON GOWEY COLLECTION (BELOW) No. 22 at the end of the Fruitvale Line near Powerhouse Road. — ROBERT S. WILSON COLLECTION

During the 1920's the J. G. Brill Company of Philadelphia was among the leaders in the development of more modern streetcars to meet the competitive threats of buses. Brill's *Master Units* were easily the most successful of the improved car designs that preceded the PCC streamliner cars. (ABOVE) Car No. 21 rolls along Pine Street. — WILL WHITTAKER (CENTER) No. 20 on Yakima Avenue in the early 1930's. (LOWER LEFT) Interior of a *Master Unit*. The curtain was to shield the motorman from car interior lights at night. — BOTH LAWTON GOWEY

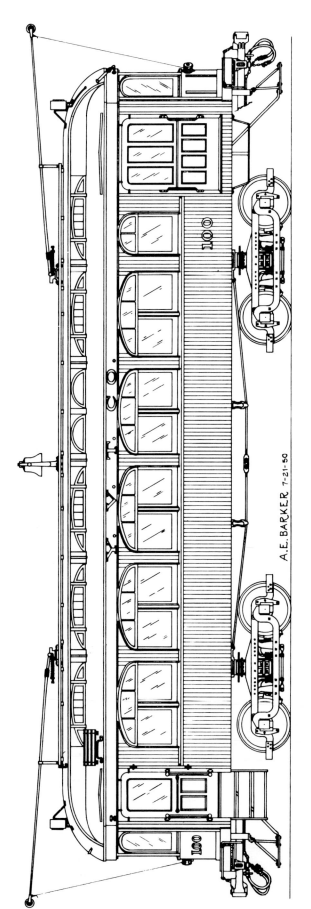

A.E. BARKER 7-21-50

Yakima Valley Transportation Company
Interurban Car No. 100

Scale Drawing by A. E. Barker

Builder - Niles Car & Manufacturing Co.
Date Built - 1909
Length Overall - 45 feet
Width Overall - 9 feet
Height Overall - 12 feet 9 inches
Wheel Diameter - 34 inches
Trucks - Standard C-50
Motors - 4 General Electric 80
Controls - K-28-F
Horsepower - 80 h.p.
Total Weight - 40,000 pounds
Seats - 38

Scale - 3/16 inch to the foot

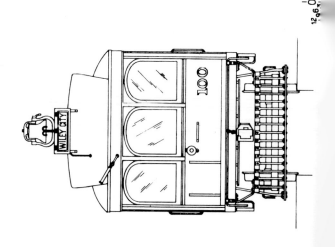

INTERIOR PLAN

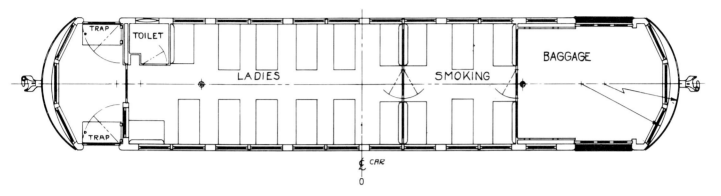

The Niles Car & Mfg. Co. of Niles, Ohio, built car No. 100 for the YVT in 1909 to open base interurban service. This car had the provision of a compartment for express and baggage in one end of the car. Thus a single unit enabled interurban operators to provide varied services. With the abandonment of interurban service, this car was retired to maintenance service.

At the left, No. 100 in the Yakima yards, not long after the abandonment of interurban service. — CHARLES SMALLWOOD (BELOW) Niles Car Co. catalog view of Yakima Valley No. 100 without its electrical equipment. — A. E. BARKER

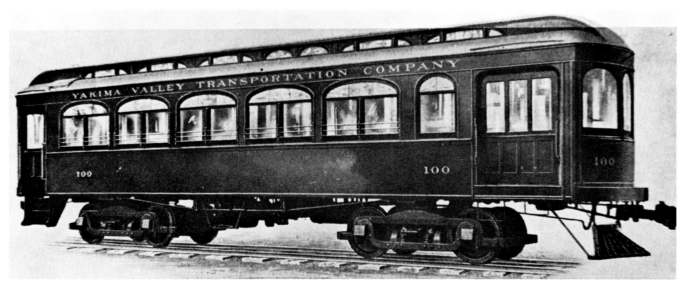

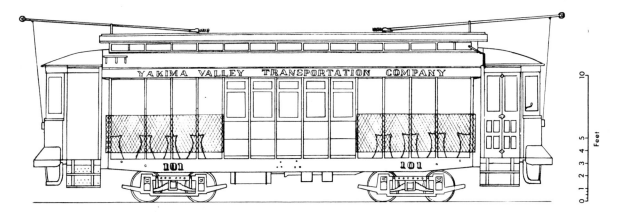

Sightseeing Car No. 101

For sightseeing service over its entire system the Yakima Valley Transportation Company ordered a double-ended double-truck convertible car from the American Car Co. in 1910. In order to obviate the high cost of a summer and winter car, the side panels and windows could be removed and stored when a completely open car was required. Car No. 101 was dubbed the *Seeing Yakima Car* and was available for private charters and outings. This car had nearly the same power as interurban No. 100, but was a couple of feet shorter in length. Its interior was handsomely outfitted in oak with brass fixtures. (BELOW) A builder's view of the No. 101 at the American Car Co. — KENNETH G. JOHNSEN COLLECTION

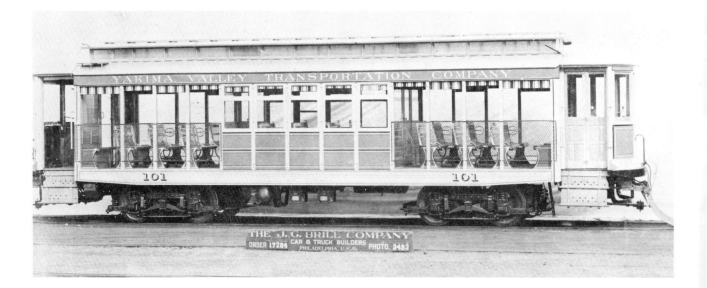

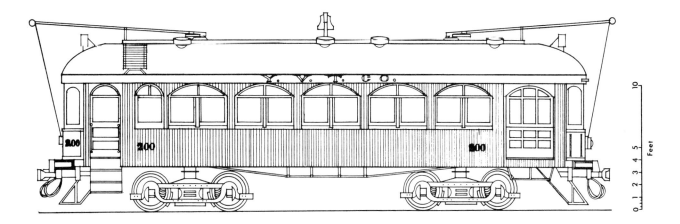

Interurban Cars Nos. 200 - 201

With the construction of the interurban line to Selah, and Speyers extension, two additional interurban cars were required to provide service on all of the three interurban routes. The two new cars were ordered from the Jewett Car Company of Newark, Ohio. These cars were nearly identical to car No. 100. Nos. 200 and 201 saw service all through the interurban era and were then placed in storage at the Yakima yard. Here they began to weather and soon showed their age. Both cars were scrapped during October of 1939.

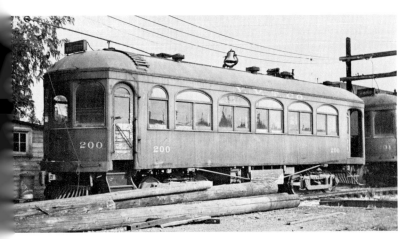

Interurban No. 200 did not appear to be in very bad shape as she patiently awaited her fate. Paint was beginning to peel on the door and steps. — WILL WHITTAKER (LOWER) The car side exposed to the sun most of the day was beginning to show wear and tear. The front pilot had disappeared and the roof probably leaked. — CHARLES SMALL-WOOD

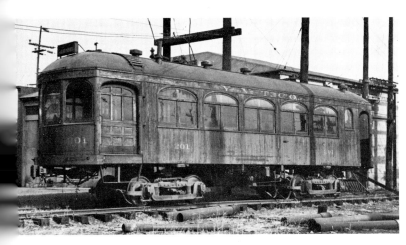

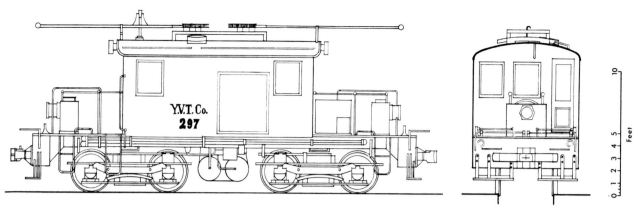

Electric Locomotive No. 297

Glendale & Montrose No. 22, present day YVT No. 297, in service in Glendale, California, in 1924. The engine saw much service as the road had a number of industrial customers. — DONALD DUKE COLLECTION

Baldwin-Westinghouse electric locomotives were the combined product of the Baldwin Locomotive Works, a pioneer steam locomotive builder, and Westinghouse Electric & Mfg. Co., the leading maker of heavy electric railway power appliances. This 50-ton switcher was built for the Glendale & Montrose in 1923 and used to switch industrial sidings on the interurban line. Upon abandonment of the road, the Union Pacific purchased the switching rights and the engine became Union Pacific E-100. When the UP changed this line to diesel, the YVT, a UP property, purchased the engine in 1942 and brought it to Yakima. The engine is presently in standby service.

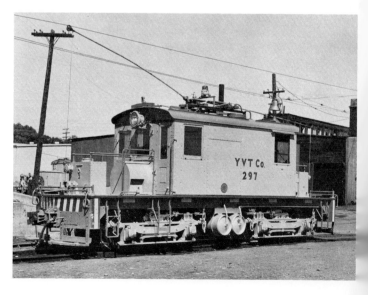

YVT No. 297 as it appeared in the 1940's. The words "Union Pacific - LA&SL - E-100" can be seen through the black paint. — AL FARROW (RIGHT) The engine as it appears today in Union Pacific yellow with red and gray trim. — KENNETH G. JOHNSEN

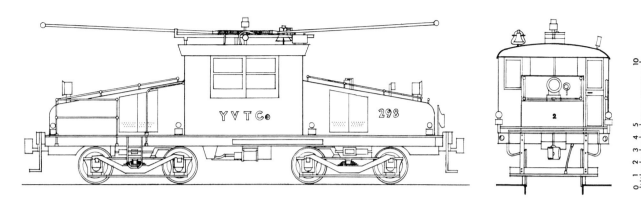

Electric Locomotive No. 298

The General Electric Company was formed at Schenectady, New York, in 1892 by combining Edison General Electric with the Thomson-Houston Co. In 1893 the firm exhibited the first commercial electric locomotive which was sold to the Manufacturers Railroad of New Haven. The firm soon became a major supplier of motors and controls for electric street car and interurban builders. The YVT No. 298 was purchased new from General Electric in 1922 and the engine is still in operation. The cab and truck frames were built by the American Locomotive Company, with General Electric supplying all the electrical parts of the engine.

Builder's view of Yakima Valley Transportation Co. No. 298 at the Erie Works of General Electric, the plant that built all the electric engines. — DONALD DUKE COLLECTION (UPPER RIGHT) Ever wonder what was under the "hoods" of a steeple cab? Air reservoir and compressor occupy most of the space. — JOHN L. AINSWORTH (RIGHT) No. 298 in Union Pacific yellow switching the apple warehouses of Selah, Washington, in 1972. — FRED SCHNEIDER

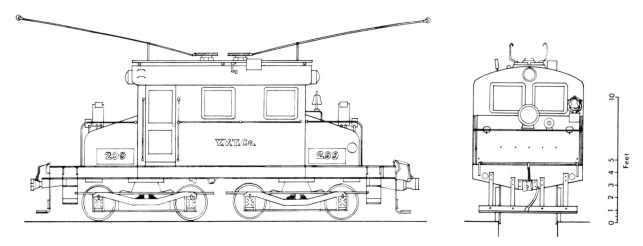

Electric Locomotive No. 299

Yakima Valley No. 299 was built in 1907 for the United Railways of Oregon as their No. 1. With their lack of sufficient freight for two locomotives, the United Railways sold No. 1 to the Oregon Electric where it became their No. 15 for a time. The engine was sold to the YVT in 1920. This 35-ton, class A Baldwin-Westinghouse locomotive was too light for continued service on the YVT and was scrapped in 1958.

A builder's photograph of United Railways of Oregon No. 1 which became YVT No. 299 in 1920. The switching footboards had not been attached when this record photograph was made. — KENNETH G. JOHNSEN COLLECTION (LEFT) YVT No. 299 when in active service on the road. This was the first electric locomotive on the YVT and saw years of active service. — AL FARROW

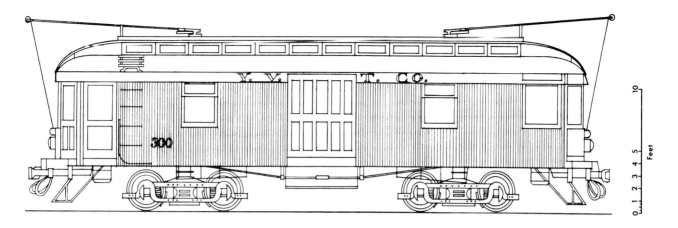

Interurban Express No. 300

An interurban express car was ordered from the Niles Car & Mfg. Co. at the same time as interurban No. 100. This piece of rolling stock would not only act as an express and L.C.L. vehicle, but operated as a locomotive until the YVT purchased a used Baldwin electric engine in 1920. No. 300 could easily handle three to four refrigerator cars of apples. With the arrival of two additional electric engines on the road, the No. 300 was placed in maintenance of way service.

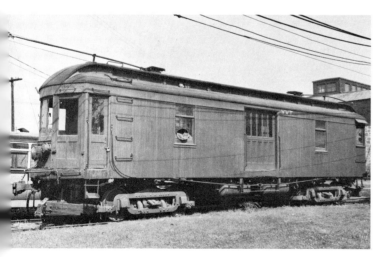

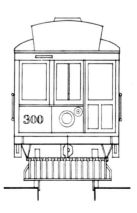

Express car No. 300 was no longer in active service when these two illustrations were made at the Yakima carbarn and shop building. The car was in pretty good condition when Al Farrow photographed her in 1946 as shown in the top picture. She had just received a new coat of paint and lettering. (LOWER LEFT) No. 300 had a broken front window and one of her side windows had a rag stuffed in it when this photo was made in 1956, just prior to scrapping. — BOB GRAY

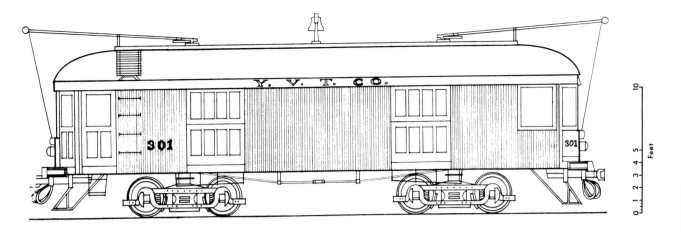

Interurban Express No. 301

With the completion of the new interurban line to Selah and Speyer's Station, an additional express motor was needed to handle express and switching of freight and refrigerator cars. No. 301 was ordered from the Jewett Car Co. in 1913 and was a near carbon copy of No. 300 which was purchased from Niles in 1909. Nos. 300 and 301 handled all freight chores until the YVT purchased electric locomotive No. 299 secondhand in 1920. (RIGHT) YVT No. 301 as it appeared on November 6, 1971, shortly before it was shipped to the California Railway Museum where it was dismantled for its parts. —KENNETH G. JOHNSEN (LOWER RIGHT) Both express cars Nos. 300 and 301 had a front door on each end of the car. — AL FARROW (BELOW) No. 301 in maintenance of way service in 1939. — CHARLES SMALL-WOOD

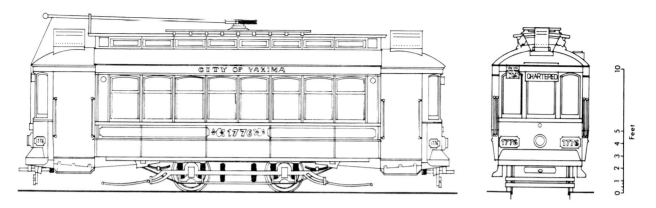

Trolley Cars Nos. 1776 & 1976

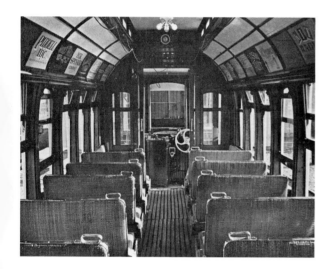

Two trolleys were acquired by the Yakima Interurban Trolley Lines from Oporto, Portugal, built from Brill parts. The No. 1776 is owned by the City of Yakima, while No. 1976 is the property of the County of Yakima. The two cars are identical in every respect. (LEFT) Interior view of the No. 1976 with its woven rattan seats and curved mahogany sides. Note the old time patent medicine style car cards on each side of the interior gratefully acknowledging businesses who had contributed to the restoration of streetcar service in Yakima. (LOWER LEFT) One of Yakima's Bicentennial beauties. (LOWER RIGHT) Motorman's platform. The handles (left to right) are the controller, reverse key, and air brake. The brass wheel is the hand brake, and the gauge shows air pressure in the reservoir. The two-way radio is below the pressure gauge.
—ALL KENNETH G. JOHNSEN

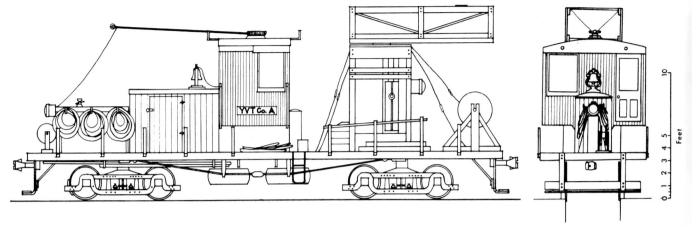

Line Car A

Line Car A was originally a flatbed electrically operated machine with a center cab. This 1909 Niles-built vehicle was outfitted as you see it here in 1922. The car is without doubt the oldest piece of interurban rolling stock in active operation in the United States today. (RIGHT) View of "A" in the Yakima yard, just outside the carbarn. Quite often a wire pole was carried on the side. — FRED SCHNEIDER (BELOW) Another view of "A" with all its various reels and rolls of copper overhead wire and stringer wire. — KENNETH G. JOHNSEN

A page from a Yakima Picture Album

YVT's standee trailers ended up hauling lumberjacks near Cle Elum, Washington.

Three-unit weedburner No. A-1 among the tumbleweeds in the YVT yard.

Yakima's first horsecar service occurred during "Frontier Days" in May of 1935.

McKeen car No. A-1 was used on YVT's Wiley City line prior to arrival of electric cars.

Twin Coaches sported a silver-gray top, dark blue band around the middle, light aqua bottom, and parent UP herald on the front.

Today the YVT has two flatcars: Nos. 1014-1015 with a boom.

Bibliography

Books

Crawford, Jeanne R., and Kay Kime. *As the Valley Was.* Yakima Valley Society for the Preservation of Early Western Americana, 1968.

Wilson, Robert S. *Trolley Trails Through the West.* Robert S. Wilson, 1943.

Articles

"Apples by the Millions." *Union Pacific Info,* October 1970.

Churchill, Sam. "Unique Traction Operations Are an Everyday Thing in Yakima." *Pacific Railroad Society Wheel Clicks,* August 1973.

Green, Ranny. "The Yakima Trolleys - A Bicentennial Preview." *Seattle Times Sunday Pictorial,* May 18, 1975.

Johnsen, Kenneth G. " 'Apple Country' Interurban." *Seattle Times Sunday Magazine,* April 8, 1973.

Johnsen, Kenneth G. "Apple Country Interurban." *Traction & Models,* November 1974.

____. "First Amtrak, Now Yakima." *Electric Railroaders' Association Headlights,* October-December 1974.

____. "In Yakima They Still Hire Trolleycar Motormen." *Pacific News,* December 1975.

"Souvenir Edition - Yakima Interurban Trolley Lines." *Yakima Herald-Republic,* October 11, 1974.

Wilson, Robert S. "Appleland Trolleys." *Electric Railroaders' Association Headlights,* May-June 1942.

Wilson, Robert S. " 'Old Yellow' Wins Reprieve." *Electric Railroaders' Association Headlights,* November-December 1972.

____. "Transit in the Yakima Valley." *The Western Railroader,* March-April 1940.

____. "Trolleys Still Pay." *National Railway Historical Society Bulletin,* March-April 1941.

____. (Untitled). *Modern Tramway,* February 1975.

____. "Yakima Valley Transportation Company." *Electric Railroaders' Association Headlights,* February 1961.

____. "Yakima - Washington State's Last Trolley City." *Northwest Trolley Railfan Group Pantograph,* December 1965-March 1966.

"Y.V.T. Co." *Pacific News,* May 1968.

Miscellaneous

"Car and Equipment Records." Yakima Valley Transportation Company, Yakima, Washington.

"Early History - North Yakima." U.S. Bureau of Reclamation (Yakima Office), Yakima, Washington.

"Mapa Das Caracteristicas Dos Carros Electricos." S.T.C.P., Oporto, Portugal.

Northwest Room Files, Washington State Library, Olympia, Washington

Transportation File, Yakima Valley Museum, Yakima, Washington.

Yakima (City) Transportation File, Yakima Public Library, Yakima, Washington.

Seattle Times Files.

Selah Valley Optimist Files.

Spokane Spokesman-Review Files.

Yakima Daily Republic Files.

Yakima Democrat Files.

Yakima Herald-Republic Files.

Yakima Morning Herald Files.

Yakima Valley Sun Files.

Index

Page Numbers in Italics Refer to Photographs

Accidents, 64, 65, 79, *99*
Ahtanum, 33
Alaimo, Ben, 100
American Car Company, 53
Apples, 47, 49, 81

Bell, W. A., 13, *25*
Bicentennial, 96, 97
Block signals, 73
"Bobbing" of Trolley Car, 57
Broadway District, 52
Brown, Wray, 95-101, *99, 101*
Buffalo Bill Cody, 25, 27
Buses, 52, 63, 64, 67, 69, 71

Cameron, S. J., 13
Cannon, Miles, 13
Capitalists, 11, 12, 19, 31
Carbarn - Temporary, 30; Permanent, 33
Cascade Lumber Company, 47, 67
Cemetery Siding, 35, 40
Circus Grounds, 27
Class, Paul, 97-100, *99*
Clogg Building, 12
Color schemes, 34, 55, 63, 79
Commercial Club, 11, 12
Congdon, Chester, 48
Convict's Cave, 45
Courthouse Loop, 33
Cull, J. O., 16, 19

Danville Car Company, 22, 31
Davis High School Band, 69
Depression, 57
Dills, I. H., 13
Ditter, P.A., 13
Donald, George, 29
Drawings, scale (*See* Appendix)
Dudley, W. B., 13

Escudos, 97, 98
Estes, J. Wallace, 63, 69
Evans, Elmer, 106
Evans, Governor Dan, 96

Fair (*See* Washington State Fair)
Fairview Line, 33, 52, 63
Fares, 14, 19
Firefighters, 100, 106
Fletcher, Doctor C. G., 16
Franchises - 10-year, 90; 25-year, 79; 40-year, 65, 67; David E. Gould, 12; Yakima Inter-Valley Traction Company, 13, 14
Fraser, James H., 13
Freight tariffs, 49, 51
Fruitvale Line, 33, 52

Girder rails, 17, 20
Gould, David E., 12, 13
Gromore (*See* Henrybro)

Harwood, 40
Hat, motorman's, *104*
Headquarters, *77*
Henrybro Line, 40
Hill, James J., 12
Hippodrome, 51
Hiscock, F.K., 13
Holdups, 52
Houston, Texas, 98
Howard, Walter, 49, 63

Jaeger, E. J., 13
Jitneys, 52
Johnsen, Doctor Kenneth G., *101*
Johnson's Corners, 18, 65
Jones, Bob, *90*

Kenly, Edward M., 42
Kennefick, John, 96, 106
Kilsimer, John, *82*

Larson, A. E., *25*
Lemon, W. L., 13
Lesh, D. E., 13
Lince, Bob, 57
Lombard, H. H., 13
Lucas, Howard C., *25*
Lucas, Mel, 71, *100*
Lumber, 47, 81

Mack bus, 52, 63, 69
Maple Street Line, 31, 40, 52
Maps - Washington State, 10; YVT Fairgrounds Loop, 26; YVT Shop Area, 74; YVT Interurban and Streetcar System (*see* Front and Back End Papers)
Master Units, 53, 57, 95, 97
McKeen gasoline-mechanical rail cars, 34
Meeker, Ezra, 27
Miles, M.B., 13
Miller, Alexander, 13, 16, *25*
Moonlight Rides, 51
Moxee, 40
Murphy, A. A., 59

Naches River, 43
Niles Car Company, 31
Nob Hill Boulevard, 65
North Coast Railway, 29, 30, 42
North Eighth Street Line, 47
North Fourth Street Line, 31, 33, 52
North Yakima, 11
North Yakima & Valley Railroad, 29
Northern Pacific, 12, 20, 42

One-man operation, 51, 57
Oporto, Portugal, 97
Oregon Railway & Navigation Company, 30, 31, 33, 42, 47, 51 (*See also* Union Pacific)

"Parade of Progress," 69
Personal service, 47, 49, 71
Peske, Otto, 106, *34*
Phillips, M. W., 13
Poem, 55
Portland Traction Company, 69
Portugal, 97
Potter, O. L. (Pat), 45, 47, 65, 69, 106, *39*
Price, Jerry, 77
Puget Sound Railway Historical Association, 69 (*See also* Snoqualmie)

Quarry (*See* rock crusher)

Rankin, George S., 16, 17, 19, 31, *25*
Reed, Walter J., 14
Richards, N. C. (Nick), 31, 42, 59
Robertson, W. W., 13
Rock crusher, 43, 45
Rose, J. H., 13
Roster of YVT equipment (*See* Appendix)

"Safe Streets Committees," 79
Sanders, Ed, *44*
Sawyer, William P., 12, 13, 15, 16, 42, *25*
Scudder, H. B., 13, 16
Seeing Yakima Car, 35, 51
Selah Gap, 42, 43
Selah Line, 42, 43, 57
Selah Wagon Road, 42
Shearer, Jack, 45
Shoot, Walt, 49, 71, 95
Shop facility, 33, *74, 75*

Signals, 73
Single-point switch, *93*
Sixteenth Avenue, 18, 65
Sixth Avenue, 33
Snoqualmie, 95, 97 (*See also* Puget Sound Railway Historical Association)
Soda Springs, 33
Speed limits, 20
Speyer's Station, 45
Splawn, A. J. (Jack), 13, 16-18, 31, 45, *25*
Steam locomotive, 33
Stock, 15, 16, 19, 31
Strahorn, Robert, 29-31, 42
Substation, 33, *76*
Sumach Park, 31
Summitview Line, 35, 52

Tacoma Railway & Power Company 17, 18
Timetables - No. 1, 23; No. 14, 51; No. 19, 58; No. 22, 61
Track maintenance, 92
Trolley Advisory Committee, 96, 98
"Trolley Dollies," 106
Twin Coach bus, 63, 64, 69

Union Gap, 29
Union Pacific, 67, 90, 96 (*See also* Oregon Railway & Navigation Company)

Washington State Fair, 27, 41, 51, 59, 63
Westbrook, 40
Whitson, Edward, 11
Wide Hollow, 40
Wiley City Line, 33, 34
Wiley, Wallace, 13
Wilson, Robert S., 53, 63; Foreword by, 7; Poetry by, 55

Yakima Avenue, paving of, 16-18, 20
Yakima Herald, 31
Yakima Interurban Trolley Lines, 106
Yakima Inter-Valley Traction Company, 13-16, 125
Yakima River, 42
Yakima Valley Central Railroad, 12
Yakima Valley Transportation Company - Abandonment of Interurban Service, 59, 63; Bus No. B-1, 52; Financial Problems, 15, 16; First Operation, 18; Flatcars, 41; Ground Breaking, 17; Organization of, 16; Roster of Equipment (see Appendix); Sale of, 31; Signaling system, 73; Streetcar Service Abandonment, 69; Trailer Cars Nos. 15-54, 41
Yakima Valley Transportation Company - Electric Locomotives; No. 297, 71, 120; No. 298, 71, 121; No. 299, 47, 71, 122
Yakima Valley Transportation Company - Express Cars; No. 300, 41, 71, 123; No. 301, 45, 71, 124
Yakima Valley Transportation Company - Interurban Cars; No. 100, 34, 117-118; No. 101, 35, 55, 118; No. 200, 45, 119, No. 201, 45, 119
Yakima Valley Transportation Company - Steam Locomotive; No. 1, 33
Yakima Valley Transportation Company - Streetcars; No. 1, 22, 110; No. 2, 22, 110; No. 3, 22, 110; No. 5, 55, 110; No. 6, 55, 63, 64, 69, 111; No. 7, 55, 57, 69, 111; No. 8, 112; No. 9, 112; No. 10, 40, 55, 63, 113; No. 11, 40, 55, 63, 113; No. 20, 53, 114-115; No. 21, 53, 114-115; No. 22, 53, 114-115
Yakima Valley Transportation Company - Work Equipment; Line Car No. A, 41, 91

Map of
Yakima Valley Transpo

Street Car and Inter

Yakima, Was

STREET CAR ROUTES

4 - North Fourth Street Line
8 - North Eighth Street Line
J - Johnson's Corners Line
M - Maple Street Line
N - South Nob Hill Line
Fairview Line
Fruitvale Line
Summitview Line

INTERURBAN ROUTES

Henrybro Line
Selah-Speyers Line
Wiley City Line

━━━ **Trackage in Service in 1979**

▬ ▬ **Abandon Trackage**

All street car routes looped around the Courthouse Loop. This loop was used as a turnaround for routes not coupled to another route. During most of YVT's street car era, routes were coupled as follows:
    N - South Nob Hill Line with Fairview Line
    4 - North Fourth Street Line with Summitview Line
    8 - North Eighth Street Line with Fruitvale Line
Interchange with the Northern Pacific (Burlington Northern) is made at Yakima via the Union Pacific connection.

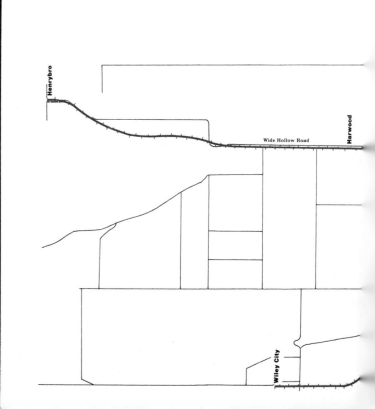